· GLOVEBOX ATLAS ·

BRITAIN

CONTENTS

Map symbols, Map pages
3

Road Maps
4-67

Ireland and Index
68-79

Index to placenames
80-96

1st edition May 1990
© The Automobile Association 1990

Published by the Publishing Division of The Automobile Association, Fanum House, Basingstoke, Hampshire RG21 2EA.
ISBN 086145 6874

Printed by Arnoldo Mondadori, EDITORE, VERONA

The contents of this book are believed correct at the time of printing. Nevertheless, the Publisher can accept no responsibility for errors or omissions, or for changes in the details given.

Mapping produced by the Cartographic Department of The Automobile Association. This atlas has been compiled and produced from the Automaps database utilising electronic and computer technology.

Every effort has been made to ensure that the contents of our new database are correct. However, if there are any errors or omissions please write to the Cartographic Editor, Publishing Division. The Automobile Association, Fanum House, Basingstoke, Hampshire RG21 2EA

A CIP catalogue record for this book is available from the British Library.

Map symbols

Atlas scale 1:500,000

8 miles to 1 inch

```
0        5      10 mls
|--|--|--|--|--|--|--|
0    5    10   15 kms
```

M3	Motorway with number
4	Motorway junction with and without number
3	Motorway junction with limited access
Fleet S	Motorway service area
	Motorway under construction
A78	Primary route single/ dual carriageway
A70	Other A road single/ dual carriageway
B7078	B road single/ dual carriageway
	Unclassified road, single/ dual carriageway
	Road under construction
	Narrow primary, other A or B road with passing places (Scotland)
TOLL	Road toll
6 M2 7 (3)	Distance in miles between symbols
TC+5h45m	Tidal constant (London). For more detailed and accurate information consult a Nautical Almanac.
V	Vehicle Ferry – Great Britain
V ZEEBRUGGE	Vehicle Ferry – Continental
H CALAIS	Hovercraft ferry
	National boundary
	Country boundary
PENZANCE H	Heliport
HEATHROW LONDON	Airport

AA	AA shops
AA	AA Roadside Shop, limited services
AA	AA Port Shop, open as season demands
☎	AA and RAC – telephones
☎	BT telephone in isolated places

QUEENS VIEW	AA viewpoint
SNAEFELL 2034 ▲	Spot height in feet
(AA)	Places with AA hotels
(AA)	Places with AA garages
(AA)	Places with AA hotels and garages

Map pages

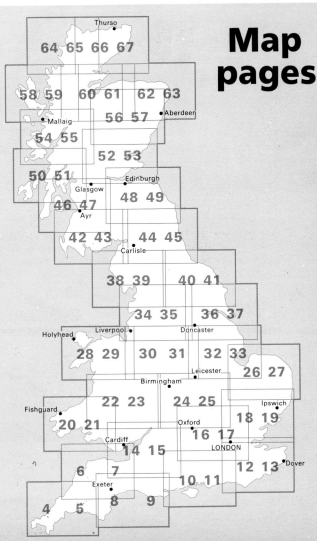

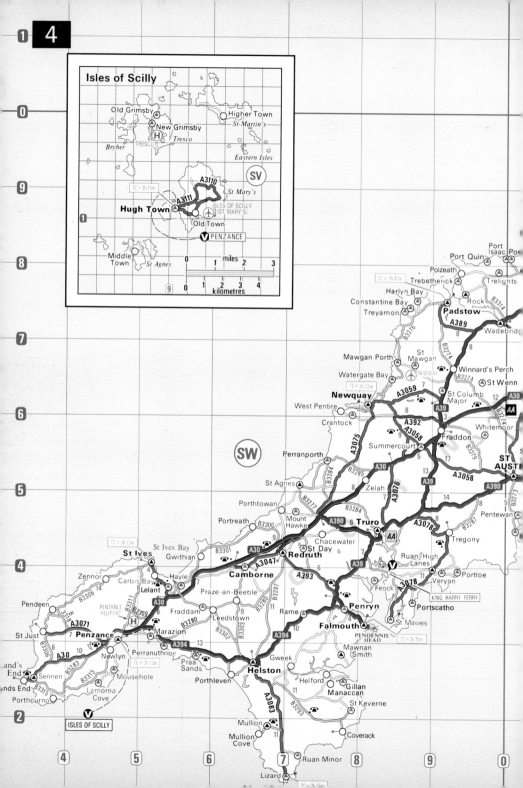

Isles of Scilly

Old Grimsby
Higher Town
St Martin's
New Grimsby
H
Tresco
TRESCO
Bryher
Eastern Isles
A3110
SV
St Mary's
TC + 3h15m
A3111
ISLES OF SCILLY
Hugh Town
(ST MARY'S)
Old Town
V PENZANCE
Middle Town
St Agnes

miles	0		1		2		3
kilometres	0	1	2	3	4		

Port Isaac
Port Quin
Port
Polzeath
Trelights
TC + 3h43m
Trebetherick
Rock
B3314
Harlyn Bay
Padstow
Constantine Bay
Treyarnon
A389
Wadebridge
B3276
B3271
8
Mawgan Porth
St Mawgan
Winnard's Perch
Watergate Bay
NEWQUAY
B3274
St Wenn
Newquay
A3059
St Columb Major
A30
12
TC + 3h33m
A392
A3058
AA
West Pentire
A3058
3
Fraddon
Whitemoor
Crantock
Summercourt
ST AUSTELL
SW
A3075
5
17
Perranporth
B3285
A30
13
A3058
A390
St Agnes
B3284
Zelah
A3076
14
Porthtowan
B3277
A39
Pentewan
B3281
Portreath
B3300
Mount Hawke
A390
Truro
A3078
Tregony
B3281
St Ives Bay
9
AA
Gwithian
Chacewater
St Ives Bay
A30
St Day
B3289
Ruan High Lanes
St Ives
A3047
Redruth
V
Portloe
Zennor
4
Carbis Bay
Camborne
A393
Feock
A3078
Veryan
B3306
Hayle
7
Praze-an-Beeble
11
KING HARRY FERRY
Lelant
A30
Fraddam
B3280
Rame
Portscatho
PENZANCE HELIPORT
6
Leedstown
B3302
Penryn
St Mawes
Pendeen
B3306
B3311
A3071
H
Marazion
B3303
10
Falmouth
Mawnan Smith
St Just
A30
10
Newlyn
A394
13
PENDENNIS HEAD
TC + 3h35m
Penzance
Perranuthnoe
A394
Land's End
B3283
Praa Sands
Gweek
Sennen
B3315
Mousehole
Helford
Lands End
B3315
Porthleven
Helston
Gillan
Porthcurno
Lamorna Cove
Manaccan
A3083
B3293
St Keverne
V
ISLES OF SCILLY
Mullion
Coverack
Mullion Cove
11
Ruan Minor
Lizard

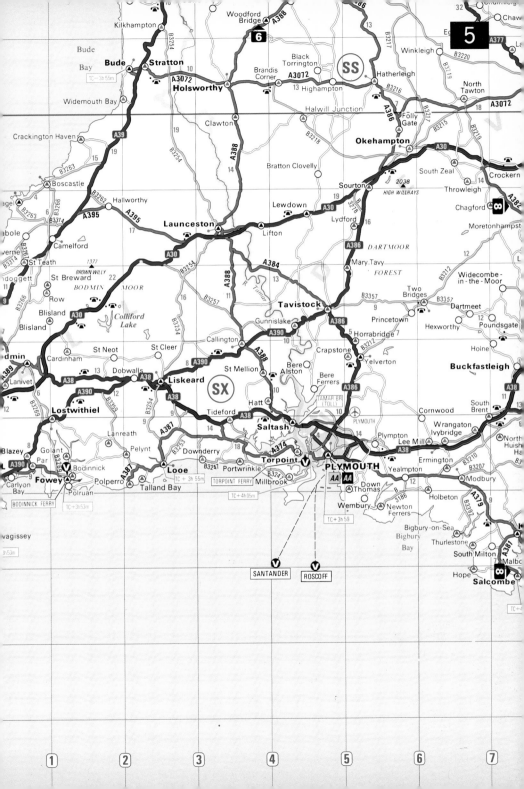

7

6

5

Lundy

SS

4

Barnstaple
or
Bideford Bay

3

Hartland Point

2

Morwenstow

1

Bude
Bay

0

Widemouth Bay

Crackington Haven

9

Tintagel
Delabole
ortgaverne

8
Pendoggett

Ilfracombe
Woody
Bay
Martinhoe
Mortehoe   Lee   Berrynarbor
Woolacombe
Combe
Martin
TC + 4h18m
10
A 399
A39
11

Croyde
Saunton   Braunton
Yelland
Appledore
Instow
B3231
A361
B3343
B3230
B3233
A39
10
AA
Barnstaple
Brayf
14

TC + 4h13m
Northam
Westward Ho!
Fairy 11
Cross
Hartland   Clovelly
B3248
Horns
Cross
Woolfardisworthy
A39
16
Bradworthy
Stibb Cross
Parkham
Bideford
Landcross
Monkleigh
Bishop's
Tawton
9
B3232
A39
12
A361

Umberleigh
B3227
B3227
Torrington
18
B3227
A386
Burrington
B3226
Chittlehamho
B3217
Chuln
32

Woodford
Bridge   A388
13
B3220
A386
Eggesford
A37
Kilkhampton
B3254
Black
Torrington
Winkleigh
B3220
Bude   Stratton
TC + 3h55m
A3072
Holsworthy
Brandis
Corner
10
A3072
13 Highampton
Hatherleigh
B3216
North
Tawton
18
A30
Halwill Junction
A386
Folly
Gate
B3219
B3217
B3215
B3219
Clawton
19
B3218
Okehampton
A30
Boscastle
B3263
15
19
B3254
A388
14
Bratton Clovelly
Sourton
2038
HIGH WILLHAYS
South Zeal
Throwleigh
Chagford
Croc
Moretonha
Hallworthy
A395
A395
17
Lewdown
Lydford
A30
19
B3218
16
SX
Launceston
Lifton
A386   DARTMOOR
Mary Tavy   FOREST
Camelford
A30
St Teath
1377
BROWN WILLY
St Breward
22
A388
13
Widecombe
-in-the-Moor
Two
BODMIN MOOR

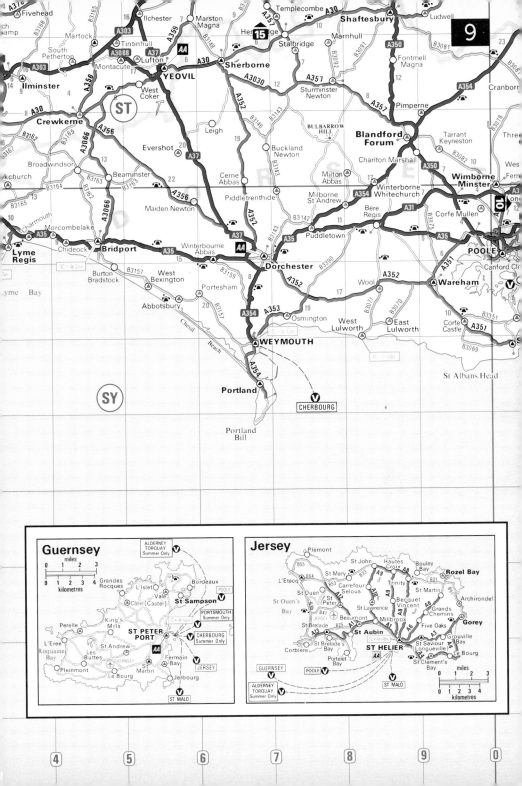

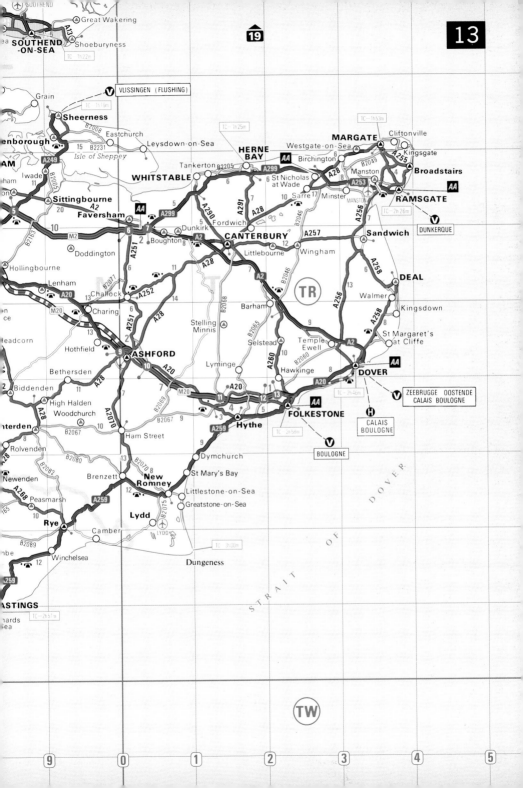

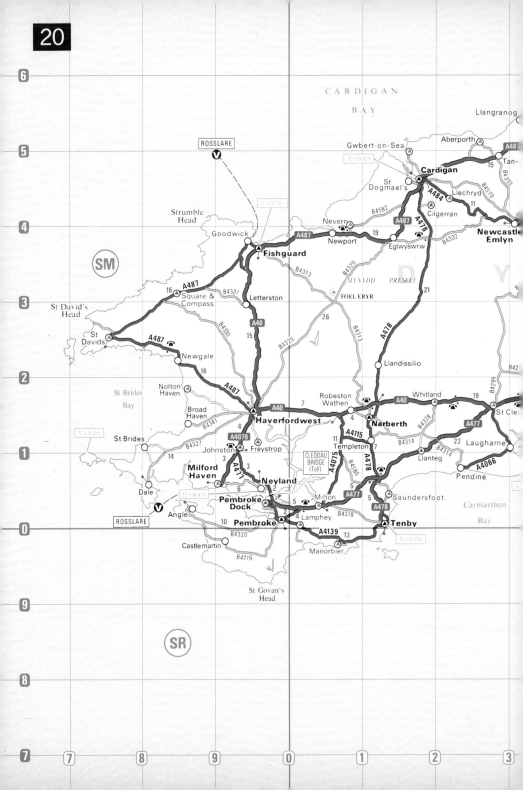

CARDIGAN

BAY

Llangranog

Aberporth

Gwbert-on-Sea

ROSSLARE

TC + 5h 42m

Cardigan

A487

15

Tan-

B4333

St
Dogmael's

A484

Llechryd

B4570

11

Strumble
Head

A487

Nevern

Newport

19

Eglwyswrw

A487

A478

Cilgerran

B4332

Newcastle
Emlyn

Goodwick

TC + 5h 45m

B4582

Fishguard

B4313

B4329

MYNYDD   PRESELI

D   Y

SM

A487

16

Square &
Compass

B4331

Letterston

FOEL ERYR

21

St David's
Head

A40

A4329

26

A478

B4313

St
Davids

A487

Newgale

16

B4330

15

B4329

Llandissilio

B4299

B42

A487

16

Nolton
Haven

A40

St Brides
Bay

Broad
Haven

A40

7

Robeston
Wathen

Whitland

A40

19

St Cle

B4341

Haverfordwest

4

Narberth

B4328

A477

St Brides

B4327

A4076

Johnston

Freystrop

A4115

Templeton

11

17

B4314

22

Laugharne

14

3

A4075

B4314

Llanteg

A4066

Dale

A411

3

CLEDDAU
BRIDGE
(Toll)

A478

B4386

5

Pendine

TC + 4h 3m

Milford
Haven

6

Neyland

2

Milton

A477

5

Saundersfoot

Carmarthen
Bay

ROSSLARE

V

Angle

Pembroke
Dock

5

5

A478

Castlemartin

10

Pembroke

2

4 Lamphey

B4318

Tenby

TC + 4h 21m

A4139

13

B4320

Manorbier

B4319

St Govan's
Head

SR

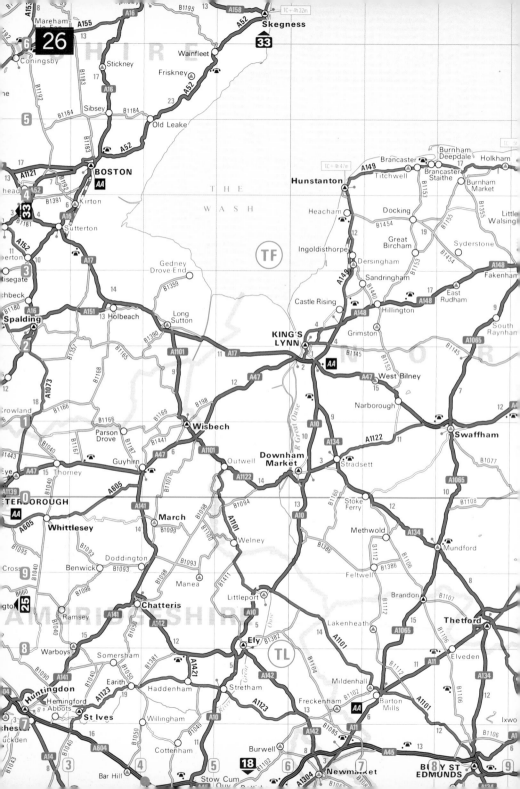

Cley next the Sea
Salthouse
Sheringham
Cromer
Blakeney
Weybourne
West Runton
Overstrand
A149
Wells-the-a
A149
B1388
B1156
A148
Holt
Trimingham
B1159
Southrepps
Roughton
Mundesley-on-Sea
Thorpe Market
B1145
Bacton
B1150
Happisburgh
B1155
A148
A1067
12
B1354
B1110
Melton Constable
B1149
B1354
Blickling
A140
North Walsham
9
A149
Guist
Saxthorpe
B1145
Aylsham
7
TG
B1150
A149
8
Sea Palling
North Elmham
11
Reepham
B1145
B1145
B1354
15
Stalham
A149
Horsey
Bawdeswell
14
Coltishall
A1151
7
Potter Heigham
B1159
Winterton-on-Sea
East Bilney
B1110
B1147
Great Witchingham (Lenwade)
14
A1067
A140
Wroxham
B1150
Horning
A1062
Hemsby
Martham
A149
Ranworth
B1152
Ormesby
A1064
Caister-on-Sea
East Dereham
North Tuddenham
16
A47
NORWICH
A1151
Salhouse
South Walsham
B1140
Acle
3
A47
GREAT YARMOUTH
Barnham Broom
B1135
B1108
AA
A47
11
Shipdham
Hethersett
A11
B1113
AA
Gorleston-on-Sea
Kimberley
Yelverton
REEDHAM FERRY
V
Reedham
A12
Hingham
B1108
Wymondham
A146
17
14
Hopton on Sea
Stoke Holy Cross
A140
Brooke
Loddon
B1136
A143
B1074
10
Corton
B1077
A11
30
B1135
Hempnall
15
Haddiscoe
B1140
A146
Attleborough
Bunwell
B1135
Ellingham
Oulton Broad
LOWESTOFT
Snetterton (Circuit)
New Buckenham
B1134
20
Long Stratton
B1332
Beccles
B1062
A146
9
A12
Kenninghall
B1113
B1114
B1134
Homersfield
Bungay
A143
B1062
A144
A145
Kessingland
A1066
19
South Lopham
B1113
A140
Harleston
Wortwell
10
Wrentham
14
A12
B1112
Diss
Scole
B1123
A144
Halesworth
B1124
B1126
Southwold
Botesdale
A143
Brome
B1118
12
TM
B1123
5
A1095
B1111
Stanton
Yaxley
Eye
Stradbroke
B1117
Heveningham
Walberswick
16
B1113
B1118
B1117
6
B1125
Dunwich
Finningham
13
A1120
Yoxford
Westleton
A1088
A140
Dennington
A1120
B1122
Framlingham
Debenham
19
Saxmundham
B1119
Leiston

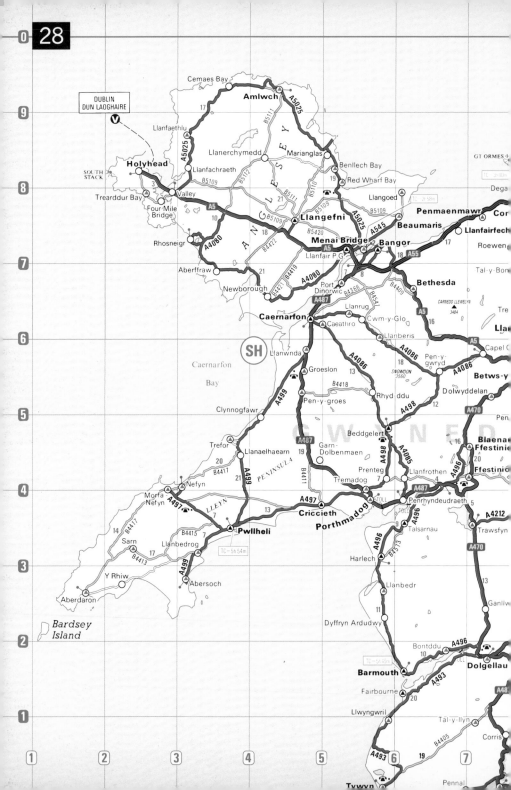

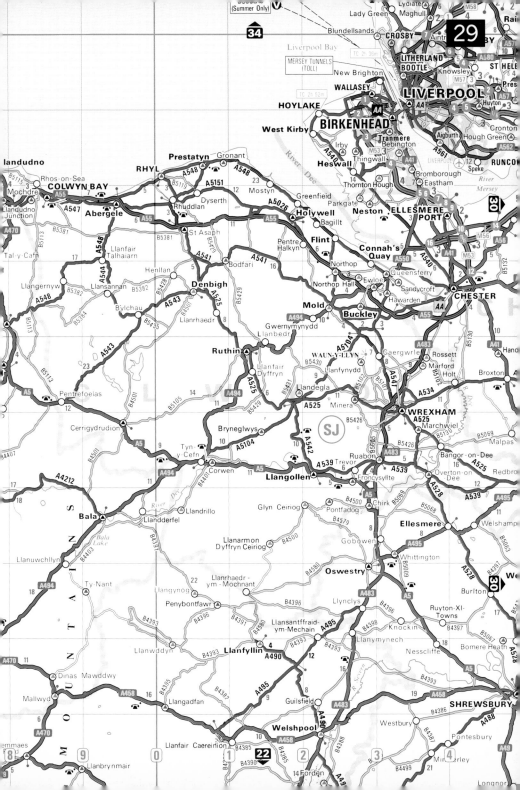

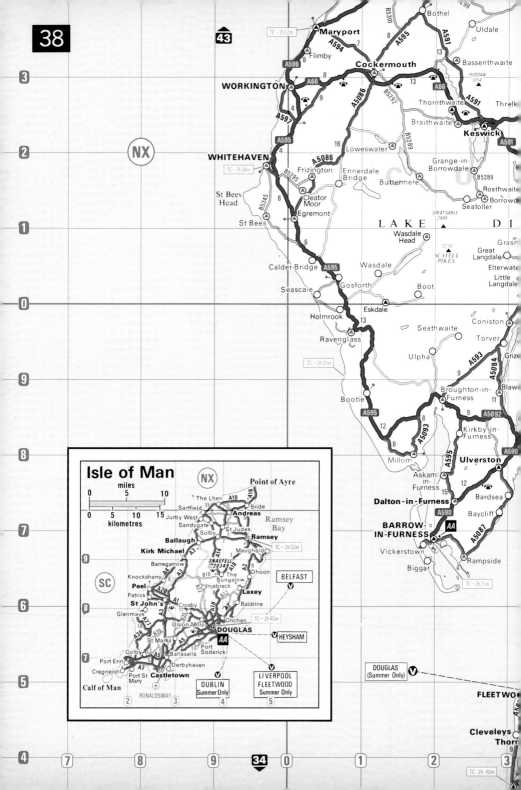

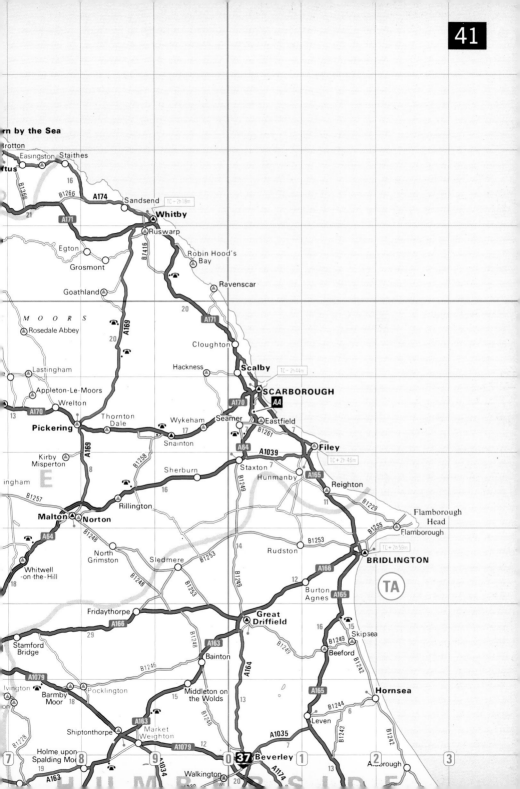

rn by the Sea

Brotton
Easingston Staithes
ftus
16
B1266
B1266
21
A174 Sandsend TC+2h18m
A171
Whitby
Ruswarp
Egton
B1416
Robin Hood's
Bay
Grosmont
Ravenscar
Goathland
M O O R S
20
Rosedale Abbey
A169
20
Cloughton
Hackness
Scalby TC+2h44m
Lastingham
Appleton-Le-Moors
SCARBOROUGH
Wrelton
A170
AA
13
A170
Thornton
Wykeham Seamer Eastfield
Pickering
Dale
17
B1261
7
A169
Snainton
A64 Filey
Kirby
B1258
Sherburn
A1039
TC+2h46m
Misperton
Staxton 7
8
Hunmanby
A165
ingham
16
Rillington
B1249
Reighton
E
B1257
11
B1229
Malton Norton
B1255
Flamborough
Head
A64
B1248
Flamborough
North
B1253
Rudston
B1253
Grimston
Sledmere
Whitwell
B1248
B1249
TC+2h59m
-on-the-Hill
18
14
BRIDLINGTON
B1253
Fridaythorpe
12
A166
A166
Burton
A165
TA
29
Agnes
Stamford
Great
B1248
16
15
Bridge
A163
Driffield
Skipsea
B1246
Bainton
B1249
Beeford
A1079
A164
B1242
Barmby
Pocklington
15
Middleton on
Ivington
18
the Wolds
13
A165
Hornsea
Moor
A163
B1246
B1244
6
Shiptonthorpe
Market
Leven
Weighton
A1079
12
B1243
B1242
7
8
9
A1035
1
2
3
Holme upon
37
Beverley
Spalding Moor
A1034
B1228
A163
Walkington
A1174
Aubrough
20

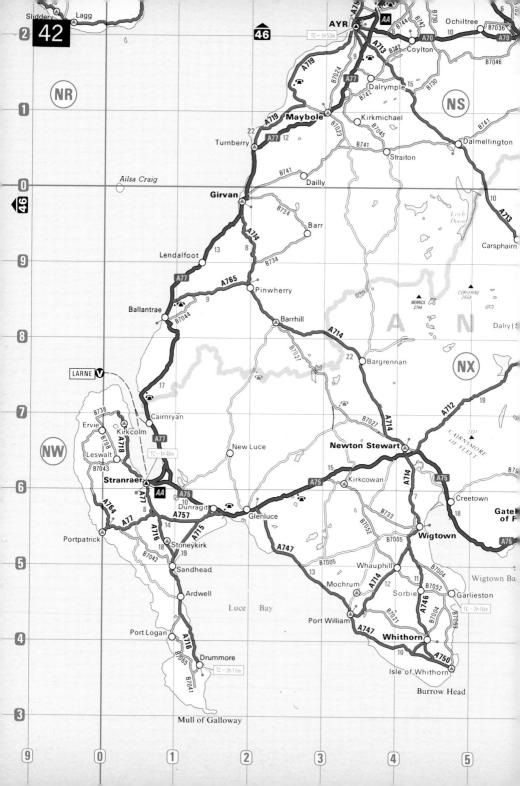

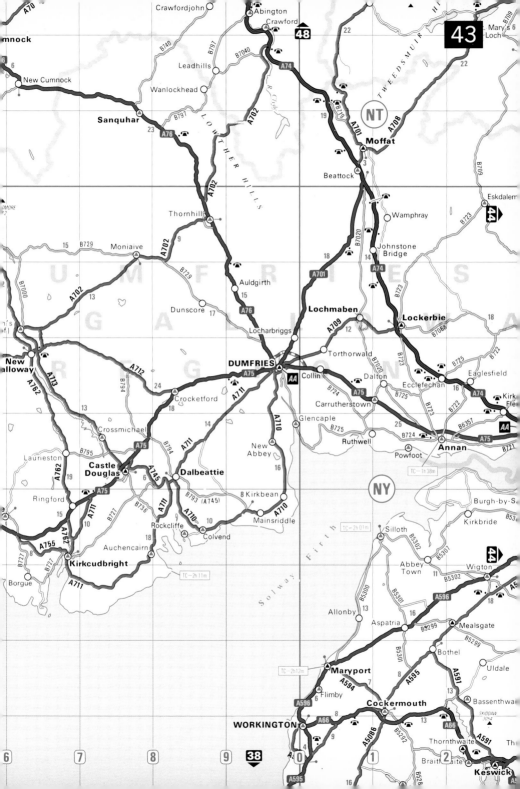

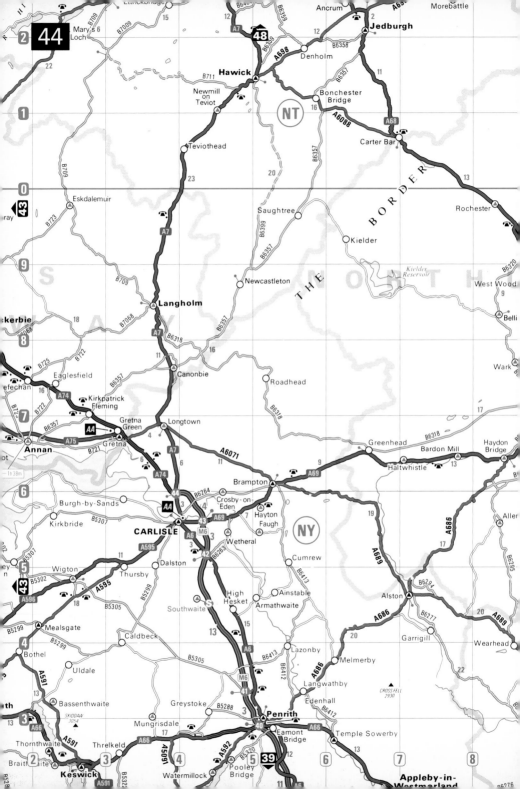

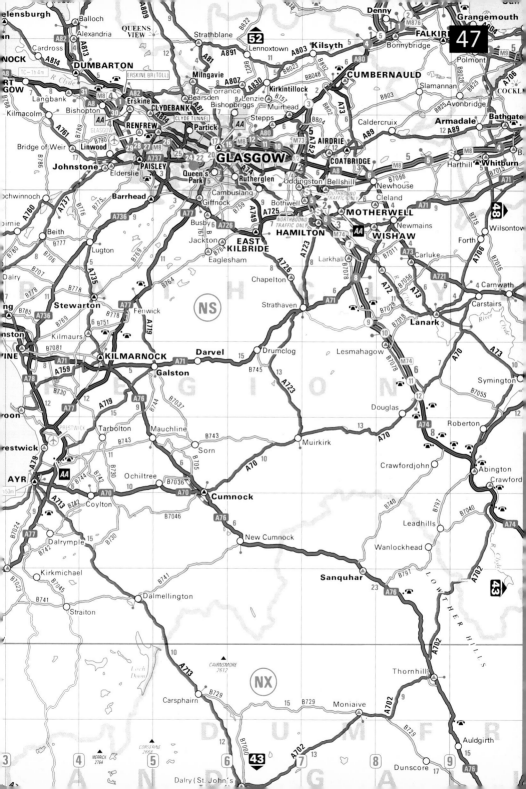

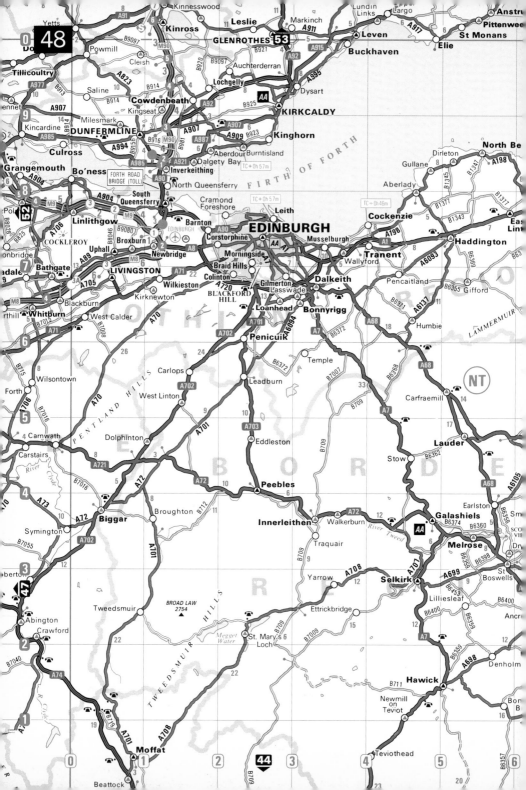

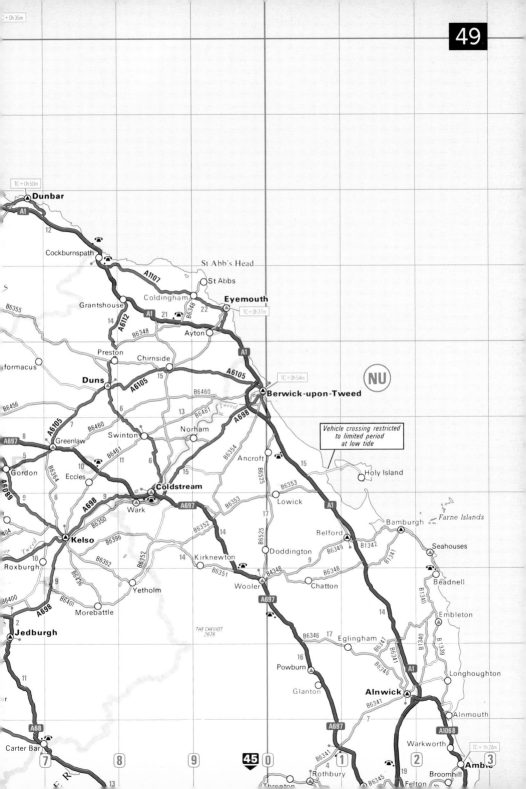

TC + 0h35m

TC + 0h50m
Dunbar
A1
12
Cockburnspath
A1107
St Abb's Head
St Abbs
Coldingham
Eyemouth
B6355
Grantshouse
A6112
A1
21
22
TC + 0h37m
14
B6348
Ayton
Preston
Chirnside
A1
formacus
Duns
A6105
15
A6105
Berwick-upon-Tweed
TC + 0h54m
B6460
NU
B6456
6
B6460
13
B6461
Tweed
A698
A6105
7
Norham
Swinton
A697
8
Greenlaw
B6461
11
6
B6354
Ancroft
15
Holy Island
5
10
Eccles
15
B6525
Gordon
B6364
Coldstream
Vehicle crossing restricted
to limited period
at low tide
Farne Islands
A698
6
B6353
Lowick
A1
A609
Wark
A697
B6352
17
Bamburgh
B6350
B6525
Belford
Seahouses
Kelso
B6396
14
Doddington
B1342
B1341
Roxbury
B6352
B6352
14
Kirknewton
B6349
9
B6348
Beadnell
10
B6351
B4348
Chatton
B1340
9
Yetholm
Wooler
Embleton
B6400
B6401
A698
Morebattle
THE CHEVIOT
2676
A697
14
B1339
Jedburgh
B6346
17
Eglingham
B6341
A1
11
16
B6341
Longhoughton
Powburn
B6346
Glanton
Alnwick
A68
B6341
7
Carter Bar
A697
A1068
Alnmouth
7
8
9
45 0
1
Warkworth
TC + 1h28m
4
2
3
13
Rothbury
B6345
Felton
Ambl
19
Broomhill

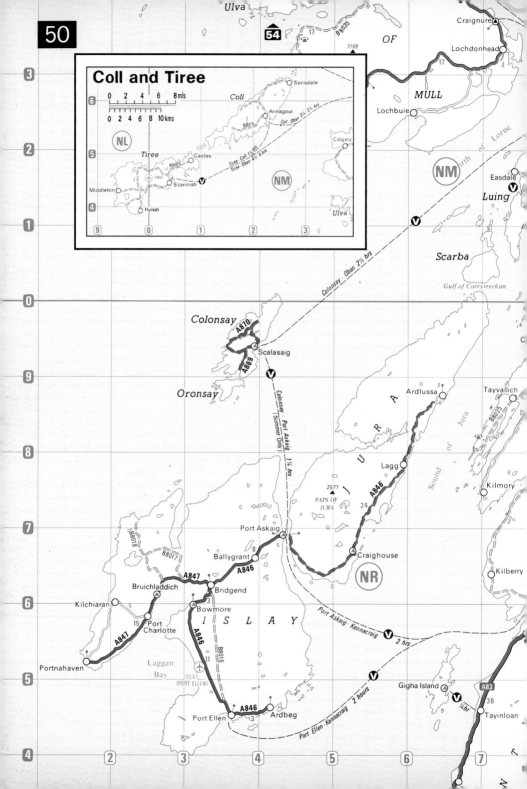

Coll and Tiree

Scale: 0 2 4 6 8 mls / 0 2 4 6 8 10 kms

NL

Coll

Sorisdale

Arinagour

B8070

Coll - Oban 3¼ - 3½ hrs

Tiree

B8065

Caoles

Calgary

NM

Middleton

TIREE

Scarinish

Tiree - Coll 1½ hrs
Tiree - Oban 4½ - 5 hrs

Hynish

Ulva

Ulva

54

OF

17

B8035

3169

Craignure

Lochdonhead

17

MULL

Lochbuie

NM

North of Lorne

Easdale

Luing

Scarba

Gulf of Corryvreckan

Colonsay - Oban 2½ hrs

Colonsay

A870

Scalasaig

A869

Oronsay

Colonsay
Port Askaig
[Summer Only]
1½ hrs

Ardlussa

Tayvallich

B8025

J U R A

Lagg

A846

Kilmory

2571
PAPS OF
JURA

Sound of Jura

24

B8018

Port Askaig

Craighouse

Kilberry

B8017

Ballygrant

8

A846

NR

Bruichladdich

A847

Bridgend

Kilchiaran

Bowmore

Port Askaig - Kennacraig 2 hrs

15

Port
Charlotte

I S L A Y

A847

A846

B8016

Laggan
Bay

3

Portnaven

ISLAY
(PORT ELLEN)

11

Port Ellen - Kennacraig 2 hours

Gigha Island

A83

A846

Port Ellen

3

Ardbeg

Tayinloan

38

¼ hr

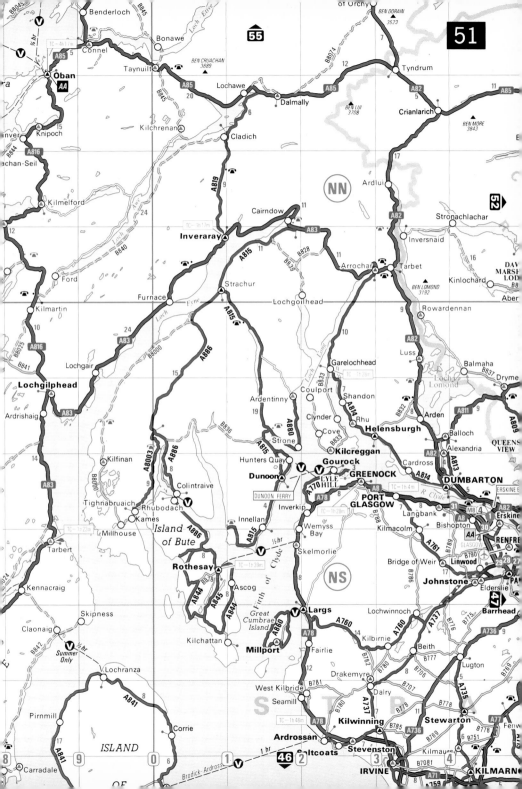

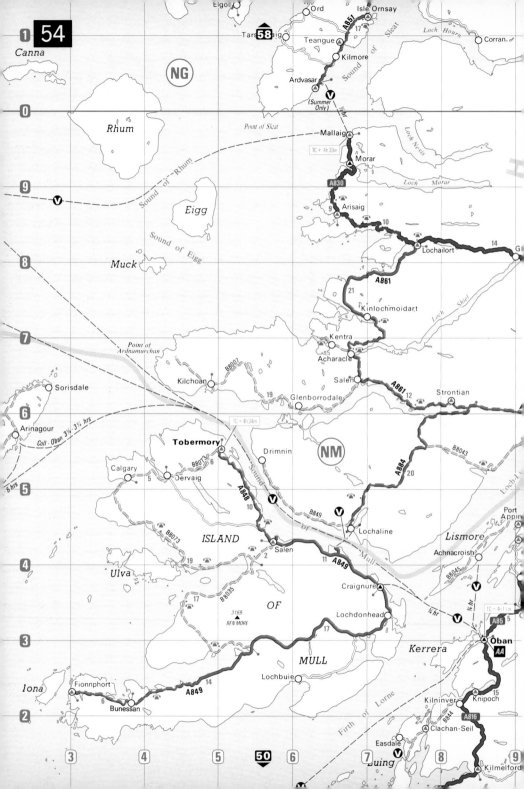

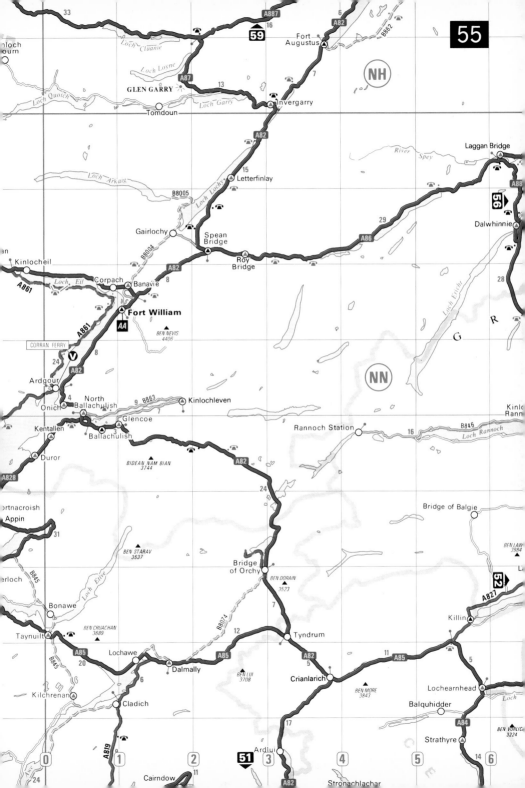

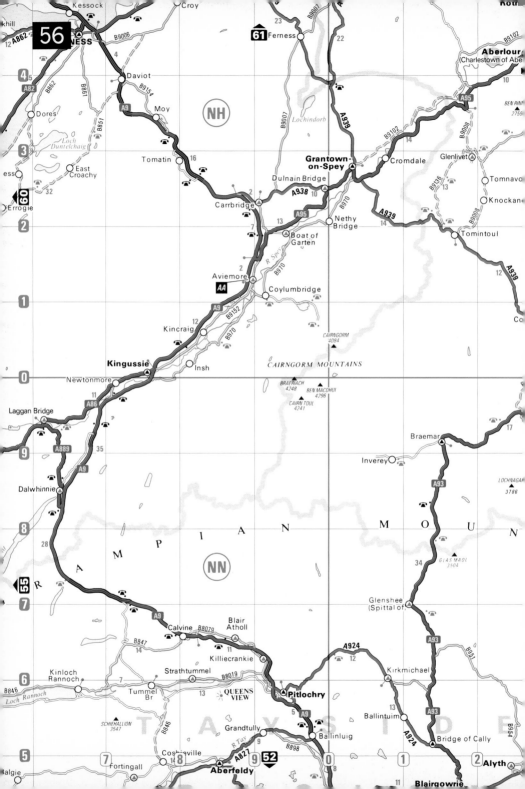

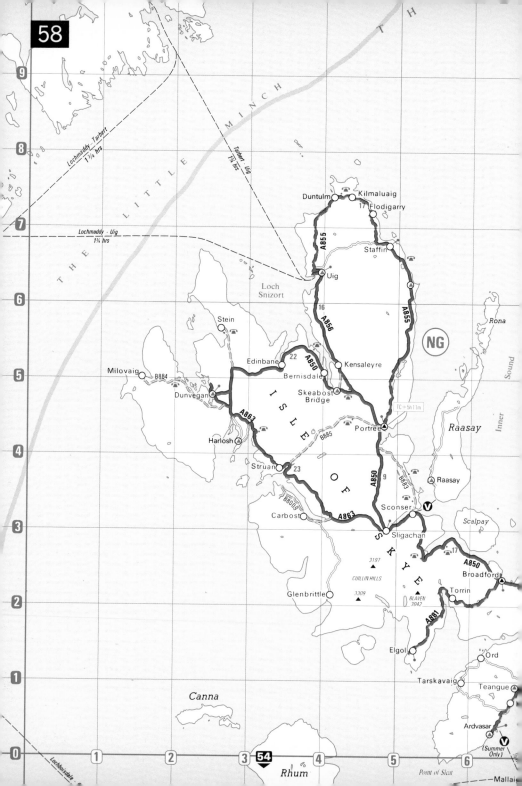

THE LITTLE MINCH

9

8

Lochmaddy - Tarbert 1¾ hrs

Tarskin - Uig 1¾ hrs

7

Lochmaddy - Uig 1¾ hrs

Duntulm
Kilmaluaig
17 Flodigarry
A855
Staffin

6

Loch Snizort

Uig

A856
16

Stein

Rona

NG

Milovaig
B884
Dunvegan

Edinbane
22
A850
Bernisdale
Kensaleyre

5

Skeabost Bridge

ISLE

B885

Raasay

Harlosh

A863

Inner Sound

Struan
23

Portree

TC + 5h 11m

4

OF

9
A850
B883
Raasay

Carbost
B8009
A863

Sconser
V

Scalpay

3

Sligachan

SKYE
3197
17
A850
Broadford

CUILLIN HILLS

Glenbrittle
3309
BLAVEN
3042
Torrin

2

A881

Elgol
Ord

1

Tarskavaig
Teangue

Canna

Ardvasar
V
(Summer Only)

0

Lochboisdale
1
2
3 54
Rhum
4
5
6
Point of Sleat
Mallaig

Canna

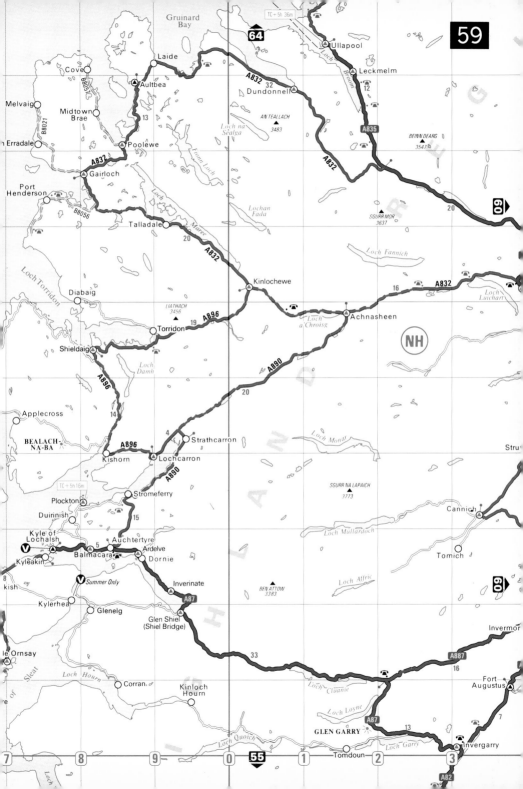

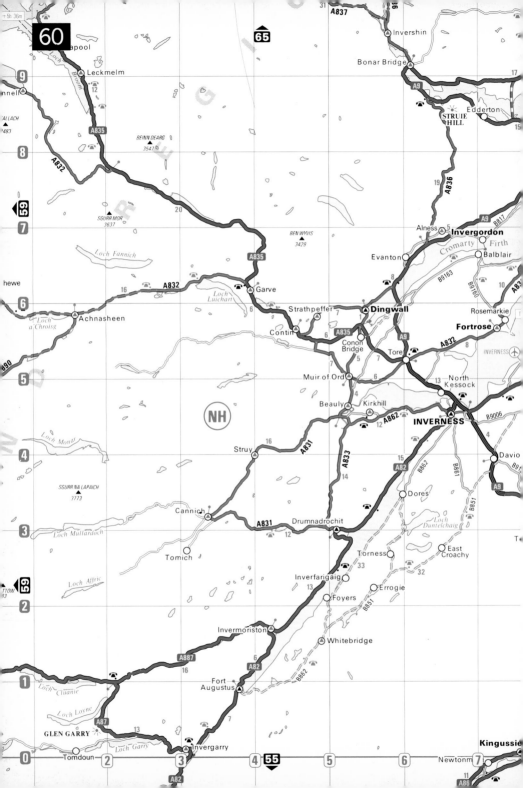

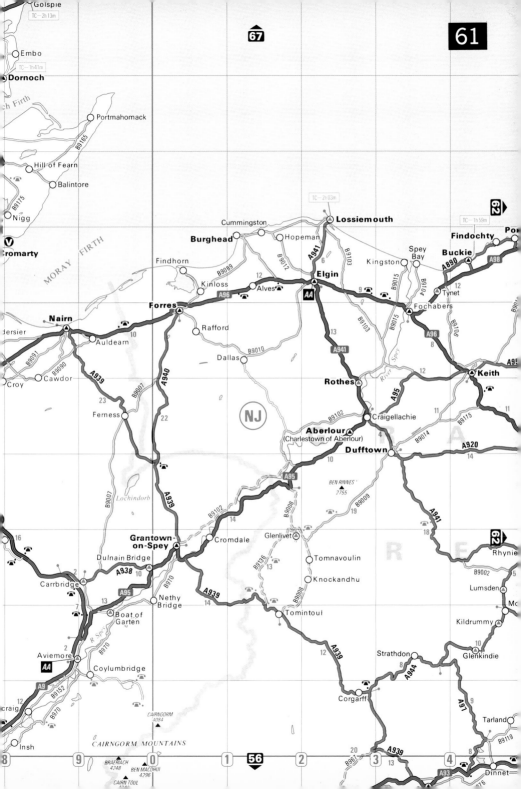

haven
Kinnairds Head
Fraserburgh
TC– 1h 21m

Inverallochy

A92

St Combs

Memsie

B9033

A981

12

A952

Strichen

18

B9093

12

A950

Mintlaw

A950

Old Deer

A952

Peterhead

NK

9

St Fergus

Boddam

A92

14

A948

Hatton

A952

Cruden Bay

17

A975

Collieston

32

n

Newburgh

17

A92

Balmedie

Bridge of Don

AA

ABERDEEN

TC– 1h 21m

A956

rtlethen

Aberdeen - Stromness 8 hrs

Aberdeen - Lerwick 14 hrs

Shetland Islands

```
0    5    10   15mls
0   5  10  15  20kms
```

Herma Ness
Norwick
Burrafirth
Haroldswick
UNST
Baltasound
BALTASOUND

Cullivoe
Gutcher
A968

HP

North Roe
A970
YELL
Mid Yell
A968
Belmont
V
FETLAR
Houbie

Ollaberry
B9078
Ulsta
V
B9081

Hillswick
11
Sullom Voe
Burravoe

B9076
Brae
A968
Laxo
V
Whalsay
Muckle Roe

Sandness
Voe
A970
Symbister

A971
Aith
V
B9071
25
KIRKWALL
TÓRSHAVN
SEYDISFJÖRDUR
BERGEN
Summer Only

Walls
Easter Skeld
Whiteness
Lerwick
V

Bressay
TC– 2h50m

HU
Scalloway

Hamnavoe

A970
Starkigarth
25

Boddam
SUMBURGH

Virkie
Sumburgh
Sumburgh Head

Lerwick - Aberdeen 14 hrs
Stromness
Lerwick 7 hrs
V

Outer Hebrides

0 5 10 15 20mls
0 5 10 15 20 25kms

NA

ISLE OF LEWIS

WESTERN ISLES

ISLAND A...

Butt of Lewis
Port of Ness — A857
Lower Barvas
Bragar — Barvas — 28
Arnol
Carloway
North Tolsta
Breasclete — A858
A857 — B805
TC+5h 19m
Tiumpan Head
STORNOWAY — A866
Stornoway
Uig — B8011
Balallan — 37 — A859
NB — V — Stornoway - Ullapool 3½ hrs
B8060

Husinish — B887 — CLISHAM 2622
Taransay
NG

Scarista — Tarbert
A859 — V — Scalpay
Pabbay — 24
Berneray — *HARRIS* — V
Tigharry — A865 — V — Lochmaddy Tarbert 1¾ hrs
NORTH UIST — A867 — Lochmaddy
Balivanich — BENBECULA — Lochmaddy Uig 1¾
Gramisdale
Creagorry — B892 — Benbecula
NF — B890
SOUTH UIST — Stilligarry
A865
Lochboisdale
Eriskay — BARRA
Barra — Lochboisdale - Oban 5½ - 5½ hrs
Tangusdale — B888 — V
Castlebay — Castlebay - Mallaig 4 hrs (Summer Only)
Vatersay — V — Castlebay - Oban 5½ - 6¾ 7¾ at night

6 7 8

Stornoway - Ullapool 3½ hrs

NB

Stoer
Inverkirka
Reiff
Polbain
Achilti
V

THE MINCH

NG
Gruinard Bay
Laide — A832 — 32
Cove
Aultbea — Dundon
Melvaig — B8005 — 13
Midtown Brae
B8021
North Erradale — **59** — Poolewe
A832
Gairloch

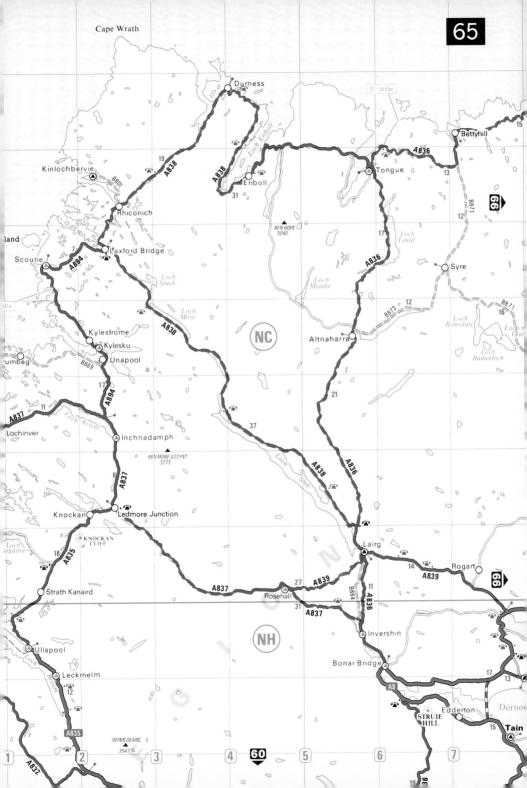

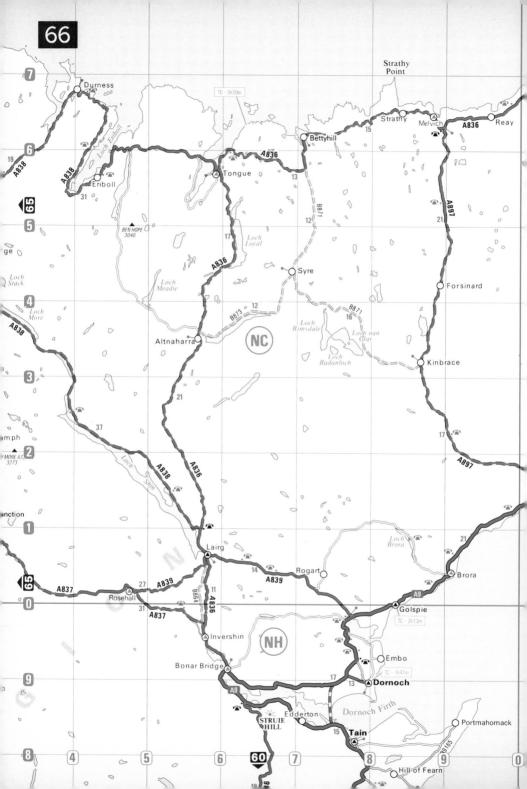

Stromness -
Scrabster
2 hrs

Burwick -
Gills Bay
¾ hr

Dunnet
Head

TC – 5h 23m

Scrabster

Thurso

Dunnet

A836

15

A836

John o'Groats

5

Castletown

Freswick

A9

A882

Halkirk

B874

16

B876

Keiss

B870

B874

B874

21

B870

Mybster

Watten

A882

Westerdale

23

WICK

Wick

A895

Thrumster

17

A9

Latheron

Lybster

Dunbeath

20

(ND)

Borgue

Berriedale

A9

elmsdale

(NJ)

Orkney Islands

Stromness - Lerwick 1 hrs

Mull Head

Papa
Westray

North
Ronaldsay

Pierowall

Westray

Rapness

Sanday

B9069

Calfsound

Kettletoft

Braeswick

Wasbister
Rousay

B9064

Eday

Backaland

Brough Head
Birsay

Whitehall

A966

Brinyan

Stronsay

TC – 3h 15m

Twatt
Dounby

B9057

Redland

MAINLAND

Balfour

Shapinsay

A967

Finstown

Sandgarth

15

Stromness

Kirkwall

(HY)

A964

KIRKWALL

Rora Orgil
Head

Houton

Skaill

HOY

Scapa
Flow

A960

St Marys

Lyness

Flotta

23

Burray

(ND)

A961

St Margaret's Hope

Hurliness

South
Ronaldsay

Stromness 2 hrs
Scrabster -

Stromness
Aberdeen 8 hrs

Burwick

PENTLAND FIRTH

¾ hr

0   5   10   15

0   5   10   15 20kms

2   G 3   5   6   7

Map symbols

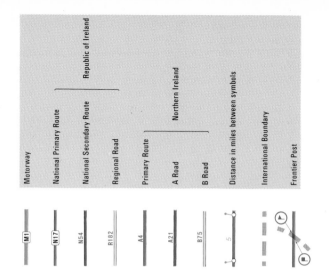

M1	Motorway
N17	National Primary Route
N54	National Secondary Route } Republic of Ireland
R182	Regional Road
A4	Primary Route
A21	A Road } Northern Ireland
B75	B Road
5	Distance in miles between symbols
	International Boundary
	Frontier Post

Atlas scale 1:1,000,000
16 miles to 1 inch

```
0        10        20 mls
0    10    20    30 kms
```

Map pages

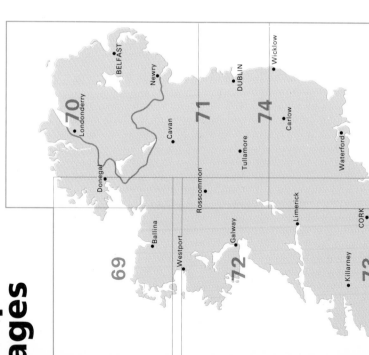

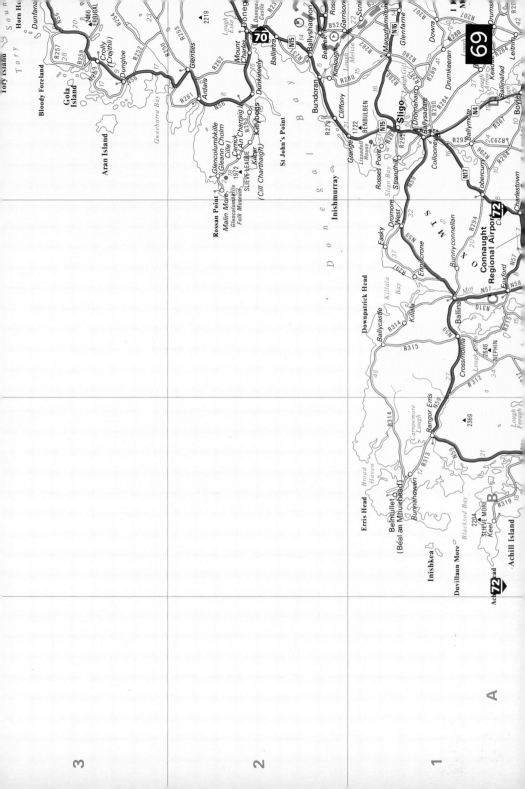

Malin Head
Inishtrahull Sound
Tory Island
Tory Sound
Fanad Head
Horn Head
Bloody Foreland
Malin
Culdaff
Clonmany
Carndonagh
INISHOWEN
Inishowen Head
Moville
Buncrana
Carrowkeel
Lough Foyle
Lough Swilly
Muff
Rosapenna
Dunfanaghy
Doe Castle
Cresslough
Milford
Rathmullan
Ray
Rathmelton
Kilmacrenan
ERRIGAL
Crolly (Croithli)
Dungloe
Letterkenny
Carrigans
St Johnstown
LONDONDERRY
Eglinton
Limavady
Dungiven
Claudy
Lifford
Strabane
Sion Mills
Clady
Stranorlar
Ballybofey
Glenties
Ardara
Castlederg
Newtownstewart
Gortin
Plumbridge
SPERRIN MTS
Donegal
Lough Eske
Mount Charles
Dunkineely
Donegal Castle
Ballintra
Lough Derg
Pettigo
Ballyshannon
Bundoran
Belleek
Kesh
Lower Lough Erne
Irvinestown
White Island Church
Dromore
Fintona
Seskinore
Beragh
Carrickmore
Omagh
Drumquin
American Folk Park
Beaghmore Stone Circles
Cookstown
Kildress
Pomeroy
Dungannon
Coalisland
Stewartstown
Moneymore
Magherafelt
Draperstown
Tobermore
Maghera
Swatragh
Dungiven Priory
Banagher
Garvagh
Kilrea
Portglenone
Gulladuff
Bellaghy
Coleraine
Castlerock
Black Glen
Portstewart
Portrush
Dunlace Castle
Giants Causeway
Bushmills
White Park Bay
Rathlin Island
Kinbane Castle
Ballycastle
Armoy
Causeway Safari Park
Dervock
Ballymoney
Dunloy
Rasharkin
Cullybackey
Ahoghill
Ballymena
Broughshane
Kells
Moorfields
Ballynure
Larne
Island Magee
Ballygalley
Ballygalley Head
Glenarm
Carnlough
Garron Point
Red Bay
To Stranraer
To Cairnryan
Randalstown
Antrim
Templepatrick
Doagh
Ballyclare
Ballycarry
Whitehead
Carrickfergus
Newtownabbey
Bangor
To Liverpool
To Douglas
Donaghadee
Holywood
Harbour Airport
Newtownards
Ballycopeland
Mount Stewart House
Ballywalter
Comber
Greyabbey
Carryduff
BELFAST
Lisburn
Dunmurry
Glenavy
Crumlin
Belfast International Airport
Lough Neagh
Arboe Cross
Coagh
Ballyronan
Springhill
Tullaghoge Fort
Donaghmore
NORTHERN IRELAND
Rough Fort

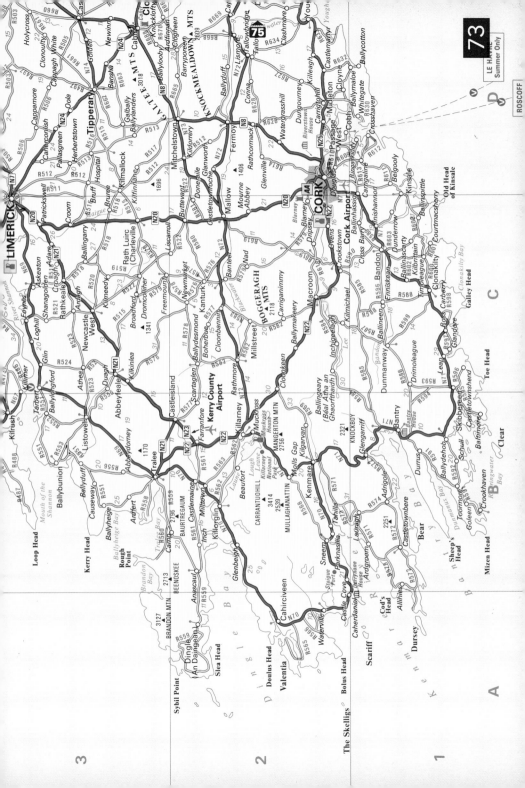

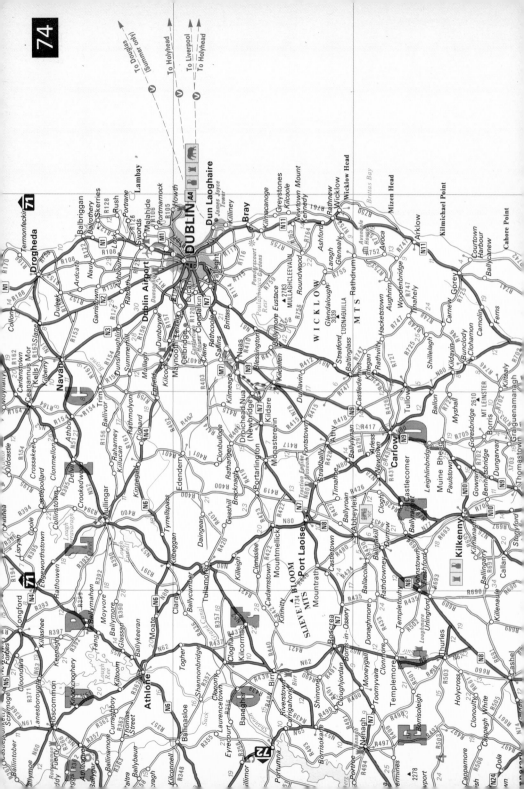

Index to Ireland

Each placename reference in the index gives the page number first, followed by the letter and number of the square in which the particular place can be found.

For example,   Belfast 70 D4 is located on page 70

Abbeydorney	73 B3	Ballindine	72 C6	Ballymote	69 D1
Abbeyfeale	73 C3	Ballineen	73 C1	Ballynahinch	71 D3
Abbeyleix	74 B4	Ballingarry	73 C1	Ballynure	70 D4
Adamstown	75 C3	Ballingarry	74 B4	Ballyragget	74 B4
Adare	73 B3	Ballingeary (Beal Atha an		Ballyroan	74 B5
Adrigole	73 B1	Ghaorfthaidh)	73 C2	Ballyronan	70 C4
Ahascragh	72 D5	Ballinhassig	73 D1	Ballysadare	69 D1
Ahoghill	70 C4	Ballinlough	72 D6	Ballyshannon	70 A4
Allihies	73 B1	Ballinrobe	72 C6	Ballyvaughan	72 C4
Anascaul	73 B2	Ballinspittle	73 C1	Ballywalter	70 D4
Annalong	71 D3	Ballintober	72 D6	Balrothery	71 C1
Annestown	75 B3	Ballintra	70 A4	Baltimore	73 B1
Antrim	70 C4	Ballivor	71 B1	Baltinglass	74 C5
Ardagh	73 C3	Ballon	74 C4	Banagher	74 A5
Ardara	69 D2	Ballybaun	72 D5	Banbridge	71 C3
Ardcath	71 C2	Ballybay	71 B3	Bandon	73 C1
Ardee	71 C2	Ballybofey	70 A4	Bangor	70 D4
Ardfert	73 B3	Ballybunion	73 B3	Bangor Erris	69 B1
Ardfinnan	75 A3	Ballycanew	74 C4	Bansha	75 A3
Ardglass	71 D3	Ballycarry	70 D4	Banteer	73 C2
Ardgroom	73 B1	Ballycastle	70 C5	Bantry	73 B1
Arklow	74 C4	Ballycastle	69 C1	Barryporeen	73 D2
Arless	74 B4	Ballyclare	70 D4	Beaufort	73 B2
Armagh	71 C3	Ballyconneely	72 B5	Belcoo	71 A3
Armoy	70 C5	Ballycotton	73 D1	Belfast	70 D4
Arthurstown	75 B3	Ballycumber	74 A5	Belgooly	73 D1
Arvagh	71 B2	Ballydehob	73 B1	Bellaghy	70 C4
Ashbourne	71 C1	Ballydesmond	73 C2	Balleek	70 A4
Ashford	74 C5	Ballyduff	73 D2	Belmullet (Beal an Mhuirhead)	69 B1
Askeaton	73 C3	Ballyfarnan	69 D1	Belturbet	71 B3
Athboy	71 B2	Ballygalley	70 D4	Benburb	71 C3
Athea	73 C3	Ballygar	72 D5	Bennetsbridge	74 B4
Augher	71 B3	Ballygawley	70 B4	Beragh	70 B4
Aughnacloy	71 B3	Ballygowan	70 D4	Birr	74 A5
Aughrim	74 C4	Ballyhaise	71 B3	Blacklion	71 A3
Avoca	74 C4	Ballyhale	75 B3	Blackwater	75 C3
		Ballyhaunis	72 C6	Blarney	73 C2
		Ballyhean	72 C6	Blessington	74 C5
Bailieborough	71 B2	Ballyheige	73 B3	Boherbue	73 C2
Balbriggan	71 C2	Ballyjamesduff	71 B2	Borris	74 B4
Balla	72 C6	Ballykeeran	71 A1	Borris-in-Ossory	74 A5
Ballacolla	74 B4	Ballylanders	73 D3	Borrisokane	72 D4
Ballaghaderreen	72 D6	Ballylongford	73 B3	Borrisoleigh	74 A4
Ballina	72 D4	Ballylooby	75 A3	Boyle	72 D6
Ballina	69 C1	Ballylynan	74 B5	Bracknagh	74 B5
Ballinafed	69 D1	Ballymahon	71 A2	Bray	74 C5
Ballinagh	71 B2	Ballymakeery	73 C2	Bridgetown	75 C3
Ballinakill	74 B4	Ballymaloe	73 D1	Brittas	74 C5
Ballinalee	71 A2	Ballymena	70 C4	Broadford	72 D4
Ballinamallard	71 B3	Ballymoe	72 D6	Broadford	73 C3
Ballinamore	72 D5	Ballymoney	70 C5	Broughshane	70 C4
Ballinascarty	73 C1	Ballymore	71 A1	Bruff	73 D3
Ballinasloe	72 D5	Ballymore Eustace	74 C5	Bruree	73 C3

Bunclody 74 C4
Buncrana 70 B5
Bundoran 69 D2
Bunmahon 75 B3
Bunnahowen 69 B1
Bunnyconnellan 69 C1
Bushmills 70 C5
Butler's Bridge 71 B3
Buttevant 73 C2
Cadamstown 74 A5
Caherconlish 73 D3
Caherdaniel 73 A2
Cahir 75 A3
Cahirciveen 73 A2
Caledon 71 C3
Callan 74 B4
Caltra 72 D5
Camolin 74 C4
Camp 73 B2
Cappagh White 73 D3
Cappamore 73 D3
Cappoquin 75 A3
Carlanstown 71 B2
Carlingford 71 C3
Carlow 74 B4
Carndonagh 70 B5
Carnew 74 C4
Carnlough 70 D5
Carracastle 72 C6
Carrick (An Charraig) 69 D2
Carrickfergus 70 D4
Carrickmacross 71 C2
Carrickmore 70 B4
Carrick-on-Shannon 71 A2
Carrick-on-Suir 75 B3
Carrigahorig 72 D4
Carrigaline 73 D1
Carrigallen 71 B2
Carriganimmy 73 C2
Carrigans 70 B5
Carrigtohill 73 D2
Carrowkeel 70 B5
Carryduff 70 D4
Cashel 74 A4
Castlebar 72 C6
Castlebellingham 71 C2
Castleblayney 71 C3
Castlebridge 75 C3
Castlecomer 74 B4
Castle Cove 73 B2
Castlederg 70 B4
Castledermot 74 B4
Castleisland 73 B2
Castlemaine 73 B2
Castlemartyr 73 D2
Castleplunkett 72 D6
Castlepollard 71 B2
Castlerea 72 D6
Castlerock 70 C5
Castleshane 71 B3
Castletown 74 B5
Castletownbere 73 B1
Castletownroche 73 D2
Castletownshend 73 C1
Castlewsellan 71 D3
Causeway 73 B2
Cavan 71 B2
Ceanannus Mor (Kells) 71 B2
Celbridge 74 C5
Charlestown 72 C6
Clady 70 B4
Clane 74 C5
Clara 74 A5
Clarecastle 72 C4
Claremorris 72 C6
Clarinbridge 72 C5

Clashmore 75 A2
Claudy 70 B5
Clifden 72 B5
Cliffony 69 D1
Clogan 74 A5
Clogh 74 B4
Clogheen 75 A3
Clogher 71 B3
Clohamon 74 C4
Clonakilty 73 C1
Clonard 74 B6
Clonaslee 74 B5
Clonbulloge 74 B5
Clonbur (An Fhairche) 72 C5
Clondalkin 74 C5
Clones 71 B3
Clonmany 70 B5
Clonmel 75 A3
Clonmellon 71 B2
Clonmore 74 A4
Clonony 74 A5
Clonoulty 74 A4
Clonroche 75 C3
Clontibret 71 E4
Cloonbannin 73 C2
Cloondara 71 A2
Cloonkeen 73 C2
Cloonlara 72 D4
Clough 71 D3
Cloughjordan 74 A5
Cloyne 73 D2
Coagh 70 C4
Coalisland 70 C4
Cobh 73 D2
Coleraine 70 C5
Collinstown 71 B2
Collon 71 C2
Collooney 69 D1
Comber 70 D4
Conna 73 D2
Cookestown 70 C4
Coole 71 B2
Cooraclare 72 C4
Cootehill 71 B3
Cork 73 D2
Cork Airport 73 D2
Cornamona 72 C5
Corofin 72 C4
Courtmacsherry 73 C1
Courtown Harbour 74 C4
Craigavon 71 C3
Craughwell 72 C5
Creggs 72 D5
Cresslough 70 A5
Croagh 73 C3
Crolly (Croithli) 70 A5
Crookedwood 71 B2
Crookhaven 73 B1
Crookstown 73 C2
Croom 73 C3
Crossakeel 71 B2
Cross Barry 73 C1
Crosshaven 73 D1
Crossmaglen 71 C3
Crossmolina 69 C1
Crumlin 70 C4
Crusheen 72 C4
Culdaff 70 B5
Culleybackey 70 C4
Curracloe 75 C3
Curraghboy 71 A1
Curry 69 C1

Daingean 74 B5
Delvin 71 B2

Derrygonnelly 71 A3
Derrylin 71 B3
Dervock 70 C5
Dingle (An Daingean) 73 A2
Doagh 70 D4
Donaghadee 70 D4
Donaghmore 74 A4
Donegal 70 A4
Doneraile 73 C2
Doonbeg 72 B4
Douglas 73 D2
Downpatrick 71 D5
Dowra 71 A3
Draperstown 70 C4
Drimoleague 73 C1
Dripsey 73 C2
Drogheda 71 C2
Droichead Nua (Newbridge)... 74 C5
Dromahair 69 D1
Dromcolliher 73 C3
Dromore 71 C3
Dromore 70 B4
Dromore West 69 C1
Drum 71 B3
Drumconrath 71 C2
Drumkeeran 71 A3
Drumlish 71 A2
Drumod 71 A2
Drumquin 70 B4
Drumshanbo 71 A3
Drumsna 71 A2
Duagh 73 C3
Dublin 74 C5
Duleek 71 C2
Dunboyne 74 C6
Duncormick 75 C3
Dundalk 71 C2
Dunderrow 73 C1
Dundrum 71 D3
Dunfanaghy 70 A5
Dungannon 70 C4
Dungarvan 75 A3
Dungarvan 74 B4
Dungiven 70 B5
Dungloe 69 D3
Dungourney 73 D2
Dunkineely 69 D2
Dun Laoghaire 74 C5
Dunlavin 74 C5
Dunleer 71 C2
Dunloy 70 C5
Dunmanway 73 C1
Dunmore 72 C6
Dunmore East 75 B3
Dunmurry 70 D4
Dunshauglin 71 C1
Durrow 74 B4
Durrus 73 B1

Easky 69 C1
Edenderry 74 B5
Edgeworthstown 71 B2
Eglinton 70 B5
Elphin 72 D6
Emyvale 71 B3
Enfield 74 B6
Ennis 72 C4
Enniscorthy 74 C4
Enniscrone 69 C1
Enniskean 73 C1
Enniskillen 71 B3
Ennistymon 72 C4
Eyrecourt 74 A5

Farnaght	71 A2
Farranfore	73 B2
Feakie	72 C4
Fenagh	71 A3
Fermoy	73 D2
Ferns	74 C4
Fethard	75 A3
Fethard	75 B3
Finnea	71 B2
Fintona	70 B4
Fivemiletown	71 B3
Fontstown	74 B5
Foulkesmills	75 B3
Foxford	69 C1
Foynes	73 C3
Freemount	73 C3
Frenchpark	72 D6
Freshford	74 B4
Fuerty	72 D6
Galbally	73 D3
Galway	72 C5
Garrison	71 A3
Garristown	71 C1
Garvagh	70 C5
Geashill	74 B5
Gilford	71 C3
Glandore	73 C1
Glanmire	73 D2
Glanworth	73 D2
Glaslough	71 B3
Glassan	71 A1
Glenamaddy	72 D6
Glenarm	70 D5
Glenavy	70 C4
Glenbeigh	73 B2
Glencolumbkille (Gleann	
Cholm Cille)	69 D2
Glendalough	74 C5
Glenealy	74 C5
Glenfarne	71 A3
Glengarriff	73 B1
Glenmore	75 B3
Glenties	69 D2
Glenville	73 D2
Glin	73 C3
Glinsk (Glinsce)	72 B5
Golden	74 A4
Goleen	73 B1
Goresbridge	74 B4
Gorey	74 C4
Gort	72 C4
Gortin	70 B4
Gowran	74 B4
Graiguenamanagh	74 B4
Grailagh	72 D6
Granard	71 B2
Grange	69 D1
Greencastle	71 C3
Greyabbey	70 D4
Greystones	74 C5
Gulladuff	70 C4
Hacketwtown	74 C4
Headford	72 C5
Herbertstown	73 D3
Hillsborough	70 C4
Hilltown	71 C3
Hospital	73 D3
Holycross	74 A4
Holywood	70 D4
Howth	74 C5

Inch	73 B2
Inchigeelagh	73 C2
Inishannon	73 C1
Irvinestown	70 B4
Johnstown	74 B4
Kanturk	73 C2
Keadue	71 A3
Keady	71 C3
Keel	69 B1
Keenagh	71 A2
Kells	70 C4
Kenmare	73 B2
Kesh	70 A4
Kilbeggan	74 B6
Kilberry	71 C2
Kilbrittain	73 C1
Kilcar (Cill Charthaigh)	69 D2
Kilcock	74 C6
Kilcolgan	72 C5
Kilconnell	72 C4
Kilconnell	72 D5
Kilcoole	74 C5
Kilcormac	74 A5
Kilcullen	74 C5
Kilcurry	71 C3
Kildare	74 B5
Kildavin	74 C4
Kildorrery	73 D2
Kildress	70 C4
Kilfenora	72 C4
Kilfinnane	73 D3
Kilgarvan	73 B2
Kilkee	72 B4
Kilkeel	71 D3
Kilkelly	72 C6
Kilkenny	74 B4
Kilkieran (Cill Ciarain)	72 B5
Kilkinlea	73 C3
Kill	75 B3
Killadysert	73 C3
Killala	69 C1
Killaloe	72 D4
Killarney	73 B2
Killashandra	71 B3
Killashee	71 A2
Killeagh	75 A2
Killenaule	74 A4
Killimor	73 C3
Killimor	72 D4
Killiney	74 C5
Killinick	75 C3
Killorglin	73 B2
Killough	71 D3
Killucan	71 B1
Killybegs	69 D2
Killyleagh	71 D3
Kilmaconoge	74 C5
Kilmacrenan	70 A5
Kilmacthomas	75 B3
Kilmaganny	75 B3
Kilmaine	72 C6
Kilmallock	73 D3
Kilmanagh	74 B4
Kilmanahan	75 A3
Kilmeaden	75 B3
Kilmeage	74 B5
Kilmeedy	73 C3
Kilmichael	73 C2
Kilmore Quay	75 C3
Kilnalech	71 B2
Kilrea	70 C5
Kilrush	73 B3

Kilsheelan	75 A3
Kiltealy	74 C4
Kiltegan	74 C4
Kiltimagh	72 C6
Kiltoom	71 A1
Kingscourt	71 C2
Kinlough	69 D1
Kinnegad	74 B6
Kinnitty	74 A5
Kinsale	73 D1
Kinvarra	72 C4
Kircubbin	70 D4
Knock	72 C6
Knockcroghery	71 A2
Knocklofty	75 A3
Knockmahon	75 B3
Knocktopher	74 B4
Lahinch	72 C4
Lanesborough	71 A2
Laragh	74 C5
Larne	70 D4
Lauragh	73 B1
Laurencetown	72 D5
Leap	73 C1
Leenene	72 B6
Leighlinbridge	74 B4
Leitrim	71 A3
Leixlip	74 C5
Lemybrien	75 A3
Letterfrack	72 B6
Letterkenny	70 B5
Lifford	70 B4
Limavady	70 B5
Limerick	73 C3
Lisbellaw	71 B3
Lisburn	70 C4
Liscarroll	73 C2
Lisdoonvarna	72 C4
Lismore	75 A3
Lisnaskea	71 B3
Lisryan	71 B2
Listowel	73 B3
Loghill	73 C3
Londonderry	70 B5
Longford	71 A2
Loughbrickland	71 C3
Loughgall	71 C3
Loughglinn	72 D6
Loughrea	72 D5
Louisburgh	72 B6
Lucan	74 C5
Lurgan	70 C4
Lusk	71 C1
Macroom	73 C2
Maghera	71 D3
Maghera	70 C4
Magherafeld	70 C4
Maguiresbridge	71 B3
Malahide	74 C6
Malin	70 B5
Malin More	69 D2
Mallow	73 C2
Manorhamilton	71 A3
Markethill	71 C3
Maynooth	74 C6
Maze	70 C4
Middletown	71 C3
Midleton	73 D2
Milford	70 B5
Millstreet	73 C2
Milltown	73 B2
Milltown Malbay	72 C4

Mitchelstown........................ 73 D2
Moate................................. 74 A6
Mohill................................. 71 A2
Molls Gap............................ 73 B2
Monaghan 71 B3
Monasterevin 74 B5
Moneygall........................... 74 A4
Moneymore......................... 70 C4
Monivea 72 C5
Mooncoin 75 B3
Moorfields 70 C4
Mount Bellew..................... 72 D5
Mount Charles.................... 70 A4
Mountmellick 74 B5
Mountrath........................... 74 B5
Mountshannon 72 D4
Mourne Abbey 73 C2
Moville............................... 70 B5
Moy.................................... 71 C3
Moylett............................... 71 B2
Moynalty 71 B2
Moyvore.............................. 71 A1
Muckross............................ 73 B2
Muff................................... 70 B5
Muine Bheag....................... 74 B4
Mullabohy 71 C2
Mullagh.............................. 74 C6
Mullinavat........................... 75 B3
Mullingar 71 B1
Myshall............................... 74 B4

Naas.................................. 74 C5
Nad.................................... 73 C2
Naul................................... 71 C1
Navan 71 C2
Neale.................................. 72 C5
Nenagh 72 D4
Newbliss 71 B3
Newcastle 71 D3
Newcastle West.................. 73 C3
Newinn 75 A3
Newmarket.......................... 73 C2
Newmarket-on-Fergus 72 C4
Newport.............................. 73 D3
Newport.............................. 72 C6
New Ross............................ 75 B3
Newry................................. 71 C3
Newtown 74 B4
Newtownabbey 70 D4

Oilgate 75 C3
Oldcastle............................ 71 B2
Omagh 70 B4
Omeath 71 C3
Oola................................... 73 D3
Oranmore 72 C5
Oughterard 72 C5
Ovens................................. 73 C2

Pallasgreen 73 D3
Parknasilla.......................... 73 B2
Partry................................. 72 C6
Passage East....................... 75 B3
Passage West...................... 73 D2
Patrickswell 73 C3
Paulstown........................... 74 B4
Pettigo 70 A4
Plumbridge 70 B4
Pomeroy 70 B4
Portadown 71 C3
Portaferry 71 D3
Portarlington 74 C5
Portavogie 71 D3
Portglenone 70 C4

Port Laoise......................... 74 B5
Portmarnock 74 C6
Portrane 71 C1
Portroe............................... 72 D4
Portrush 70 C5
Portstewart......................... 70 C5
Portumna 72 D4
Poyntzpass 71 C3

Raharney............................ 71 B1
Randalstown........................ 70 C4
Rasharkin........................... 70 C5
Rathangen 74 B5
Rathcoole 74 C5
Rathcormack 73 D2
Rathdowney......................... 74 A4
Rathdrum............................ 74 C4
Rathfriland 71 C3
Rathkeale 73 C3
Rath Luric (Charleville).......... 73 C3
Rathmelton 70 B5
Rathmolyon 71 C1
Rathmore............................ 73 C2
Rathmullen 70 B5
Rathnew.............................. 74 C5
Rathowen 71 B2
Rathvilty............................. 74 C4
Ratoath 71 C1
Ray.................................... 70 B5
Ring (An Rinn)..................... 75 A3
Ringaskiddy 73 D1
Riverstown 74 A5
Rockcorry 71 B3
Roosky 71 A2
Rosapenna 70 A5
Rosebercon 75 B3
Roscommon 72 D6
Roscrea 74 A5
Ross Carberry 73 C1
Rosscor 70 A4
Rosses Point........................ 69 D1
Rosslare Harbour................. 75 C3
Rosslea 71 B3
Rostrevor 71 C3
Roundstone......................... 72 B5
Roundwood 74 C5
Rush.................................. 71 C1

St Johnstown..................... 70 B5
Saintfield............................ 71 D3
Sallins 74 C5
Scarriff............................... 72 D4
Scartaglen 73 B2
Scarva 71 C3
Schull................................. 73 B1
Scramoge 71 A2
Scribbagh 71 A3
Seskinore............................ 70 B4
Shanagolden 73 C3
Shannon Airport.................. 73 C3
Shannonbridge 74 A5
Shercock 71 B2
Shillelagh 74 C4
Shinrone 74 A5
Shrule................................ 72 C5
Silvermines 72 D4
Sion Mills........................... 70 B4
Sixmilebridge 72 C4
Skerries 71 C1
Skibbereen 73 C1
Slane 71 C2
Sligo 69 D1
Smithborough 71 B3
Sneem................................ 73 B2
Spiddal (An Spideal)............. 72 C5

Sporthouse Cross Roads........ 75 B3
Stewartstown 70 C4
Stonyford............................ 74 B4
Strabane 70 B4
Stradbally 74 B5
Stradone............................. 71 B2
Strandhill............................ 69 D1
Strangford 71 D3
Stranorlar 70 A4
Stratford............................. 74 C5
Strokestown 71 A2
Summerhill.......................... 71 C1
Swanlinbar 71 A3
Swatragh............................ 70 C5
Swinford 72 C6
Swords 74 C6

Taghmon............................. 75 C3
Tagoat................................ 75 C3
Tahilla................................ 73 B2
Tallaght.............................. 74 C5
Tallow................................. 75 A3
Tallowbridge 75 A3
Tandragee 71 C3
Tang................................... 71 A1
Tarbert................................ 73 C3
Templemore......................... 74 A4
Templepatrick 70 C4
Templetouhy 74 A4
Termonfeckin....................... 71 C2
Thomas Street..................... 72 D5
Thomastown........................ 74 B4
Thurles............................... 74 A4
Timahoe.............................. 74 B5
Timoleague 73 C1
Tinahely.............................. 74 C4
Tipperary............................. 73 D3
Tobercurry 69 D1
Tobermore 70 C4
Togher 74 A5
Toomyvara 74 A4
Toormoore........................... 73 B1
Tralee................................. 73 B3
Tramore 75 B3
Trim................................... 71 C1
Tuam.................................. 72 C5
Tuamgraney......................... 72 D4
Tulla 72 C4
Tullamore 74 B5
Tullow................................. 74 C4
Tulsk.................................. 72 D6
Turlough............................. 72 C6
Tyholland............................ 71 B3
Tyrrellspass 74 B6

Urlingford 74 A4

Virginia............................... 71 B2

Waddington 75 C3
Warrenpoint......................... 71 C3
Waterford............................ 75 B3
Watergrasshill 73 D2
Waterville............................ 73 A2
Westport............................. 72 C6
Wexford.............................. 75 C3
Whitegate............................ 73 D1
Whitehead 70 D4
Wicklow.............................. 74 C5
Woodenbridge...................... 74 C4
Woodford 72 D4

Youghal............................... 75 A2

Index to placenames

Each entry in the index is followed by the atlas page number and then two letters denoting the 100km grid square. The last two figures refer to the west-east and south-north numbered grid lines.

For example   Whitchurch 30 SJ54
Turn to page 30. The major national grid square we are looking at is SJ. The figure '5' is found along the bottom of the page and the second figure '4' is found along the lefthand side of the page. Whitchurch can be found within the intersecting square.

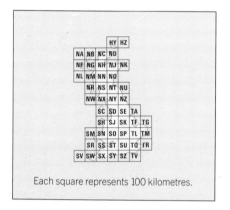

Each square represents 100 kilometres.

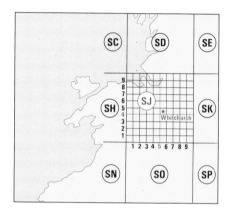

Abberley	23	SO76
Abbey Town	43	NY15
Abbots Bromley	31	SK02
Abbots Langley	17	TL00
Abbotsbury	9	SY58
Aberaeron	21	SN46
Aberarth	21	SN46
Aberchirder	62	NJ65
Abercraf	22	SN81
Aberdare	14	SO00
Aberdaron	28	SH12
Aberdeen Airport	57	NJ81
Aberdeen	57	NJ90
Aberdour	48	NT18
Aberdovey	22	SN69
Aberfeldy	52	NN84
Aberffraw	28	SH36
Aberford	36	SE43
Abergavenny	23	SO31
Abergele	29	SH97
Aberlady	48	NT47
Aberlour	61	NJ24
Abernethy	53	NO11
Aberporth	20	SN25
Abersoch	28	SH32
Abersychan	14	SO20
Abertillery	14	SO20
Aberystwyth	22	SN58
Abingdon	16	SU49
Abington	47	NS92
Aboyne	57	NO59
Abridge	18	TQ49
Accrington	35	SD72
Acharacle	54	NM66
Achiltibuie	64	NC00
Achnacroish	54	NM84
Achnasheen	59	NH15
Acle	27	TG41

Addington	12	TQ65
Addlestone	17	TQ06
Adlington	34	SD61
Adlington	30	SJ98
Aigburth	30	SJ39
Ainsdale	34	SD31
Ainstable	44	NY54
Aintree	34	SJ39
Airdrie	47	NS76
Airth	52	NS88
Aisthorpe	32	SK97
Aith	63	HU35
Albrighton	23	SJ80
Alcester	24	SP05
Alconbury	25	TL17
Aldbrough	37	TA23
Aldeburgh	19	TM45
Alderley Edge	30	SJ87
Aldermaston	16	SU56
Alderminster	24	SP24
Aldershot	11	SU85
Aldridge	24	SK00
Alexandria	51	NS37
Alford	57	NJ51
Alford	33	TF47
Alfreton	31	SK45
Alfriston	12	TQ50
Allendale	44	NY85
Allerton	35	SE13
Allesley	24	SP28
Allhallows-on-Sea	13	TQ87
Alloa	52	NS89
Allonby	43	NY04
Alness	60	NH66
Alnmouth	45	NV21
Alnwick	49	NU11
Alperton	17	TQ18
Alresford	10	SU53

Alrewas	31	SK11
Alsager	30	SJ75
Alston	44	NY74
Altham	35	SD73
Althorpe	36	SE81
Altnaharra	66	NC53
Alton	31	SK04
Alton	11	SU73
Altrincham	35	SJ78
Alva	52	NS89
Alvechurch	24	SP07
Alveley	23	SO78
Alves	61	NJ16
Alveston	15	ST68
Alwalton	25	TL19
Alyth	53	NO24
Amberley	15	SO80
Amberley	11	TQ01
Amble	45	NU20
Amblecote	23	SO88
Ambleside	39	NY30
Amersham	17	SU99
Amesbury	10	SU14
Amlwch	28	SH49
Ammanford	21	SN61
Ampfield	10	SU32
Ampleforth	40	SE57
Ampthill	25	TL03
Ancaster	32	SK94
Ancroft	49	NU04
Ancrum	48	NT62
Andover	10	SU34
Andoversford	24	SP01
Andreas	38	SC49
Angle	20	SM80
Annan	43	NY16
Annfield Plain	45	NZ15
Anstey	24	SK50

Place	Page	Grid
Anstruther	53	NO50
Ansty	32	SP38
Appin	55	NM94
Appleby-in-Westmorland	39	NY62
Applecross	59	NG74
Appledore	6	SS43
Appleton-le-Moors	41	SE78
Arbroath	53	NO64
Archirondel	9	JS00
Ardbeg	50	NR44
Ardelve	59	NG82
Arden	51	NS38
Ardentinny	51	NS18
Ardeonaig	52	NN63
Ardersier	61	NH75
Ardfern	51	NM80
Ardgour	55	NN06
Ardingly	12	TQ32
Ardleigh	11	TM02
Ardlui	51	NN31
Ardlussa	50	NR68
Ardnshaig	51	NR88
Ardrishaig	46	NS24
Ardrossan	52	NN63
Ardtainaig	51	NM80
Arduaine	54	NG60
Ardvasar	42	NX14
Ardwell	50	NM25
Arinagour	54	NM68
Arisaig	47	NS96
Armadale	44	NY54
Armathwaite	39	SD97
Arncliffe	64	NB34
Arnol	52	NS69
Arnprior	39	SD47
Arnside	51	NN20
Arrochar	11	TQ00
Arundel	51	NS16
Ascog	17	SU96
Ascot	11	SU85
Ash	13	TR25
Ash	31	SK14
Ashbourne	8	SX77
Ashburton	16	SU28
Ashbury	31	SK31
Ashby-de-la-Zouche	24	SP58
Ashby Parva	17	TQ07
Ashford	13	TR04
Ashford-in-the-Water	31	SK16
Ashington	45	NZ28
Ashington	11	TQ11
Ashley Heath	10	SU10
Ashtead	17	TQ15
Ashton Keynes	15	SU09
Ashton-in-Makerfield	34	SJ59
Ashton-under-Lyne	35	SJ99
Askam-in-Furness	38	SD27
Askern	36	SE51
Askrigg	39	SD99
Aspatria	43	NY14
Aspley Guise	25	SP93
Aspull	34	SD60
Aston Clinton	16	SP81
Aston on Clun	23	SO38
Atherton	34	SD60
Attleborough	27	TM09
Auchencairn	43	NX75
Auchterarder	52	NN91
Auchterderran	53	NT29
Auchterhouse	53	NO33
Auchtermuchty	53	NO21
Auchtertyre	59	NG82
Audgirth	43	NX98
Audlem	30	SJ64
Aughton	34	SD30
Auldearn	61	NH95
Aultbea	59	NG88
Austwick	39	SD76
Avebury	15	SU17
Aveley	12	TQ57
Aviemore	56	NH81
Avon	10	SZ19
Avonbridge	47	NS97
Avonmouth	14	ST45
Axbridge	14	ST45
Axminster	8	SY29
Aylesbeare	8	SY09
Aylesbury	16	SP81
Aylesford	12	TQ75
Aylsham	27	TG12
Aynho	24	SP53
Ayr	47	NS32
Aysgarth	40	SE08
Ayton	49	NT96
Babbacombe	8	SX96
Backaland	67	HY53
Backwell	14	ST46
Bacton	27	TG33
Bacup	35	SD82
Badmington	15	ST78
Badminton	15	ST88
Bagby	40	SE48
Bagillt	29	SJ27
Baginton	24	SP37
Bagshot	16	SU96
Baguley	35	SJ89
Bagworth	31	SK40
Bainbridge	39	SD98
Bainton	36	SE95
Bakewell	31	SK26
Bala	29	SH93
Balallan	64	NB22
Balbeggie	53	NO12
Balblair	60	NH76
Baldersby	40	SE37
Balderton	32	SK85
Baldock	18	TL23
Baldrine	38	SC48
Balfour	67	HY41
Balfron	52	NS58
Balintore	61	NH87
Balivanich	64	NF75
Ballachulish	55	NN05
Ballantrae	42	NX08
Ballasalla	38	SC27
Ballater	57	NO39
Ballaugh	38	SC39
Ballinluig	52	NN95
Ballintuim	52	NO15
Balloch	51	NS38
Ballygrant	50	NR36
Balmacara	59	NG82
Balmaha	51	NS49
Balmedie	57	NJ91
Balquhidder	52	NN52
Balsall Common	24	SP27
Balsham	18	TL55
Baltasound	63	HP60
Bamburgh	49	NU13
Bamford	31	SK28
Bampton	39	NY51
Bampton	16	SP30
Bampton	7	SS92
Banavie	55	NN17
Banbury	24	SP44
Banchory	57	NO69
Banff	62	NJ66
Bangor	28	SH57
Bangor-on-Dee	30	SJ34
Bankfoot	52	NO03
Banks	34	SD32
Bannockburn	52	NS89
Banstead	12	TQ26
Banwell	14	ST35
Bar Hill	18	TL36
Barbon	39	SD68
Bardney	33	TF16
Bardon Mill	44	NY76
Bardsea	38	SD27
Barford	24	SP26
Barford St Martin	15	SU03
Bargoed	14	ST19
Bargrennan	42	NX37
Barham	13	TR24
Barking	18	TQ48
Barlby	36	SE63
Barley	18	TL43
Barmby Moor	36	SE74
Barmouth	28	SH61
Barnard Castle	40	NZ01
Barnby Moor	32	SK68
Barnet	17	TQ29
Barnham Broom	27	TG00
Barnoldswick	35	SD84
Barnsdale Bar	36	SE51
Barnsley	35	SE30
Barnstaple	6	SS53
Barnton	48	NT17
Barr	42	NX29
Barregarrow	38	SC38
Barrhead	47	NS45
Barrhill	42	NX28
Barrow-in-Furness	38	SD16
Barry Island	7	ST16
Barry	7	ST16
Bartle	34	SD43
Barton Mills	26	TL77
Barton	34	SD53
Barton Stacey	10	SU44
Barton on Sea	10	SZ29
Barton	18	TL45
Barton under Needwood	31	SK11
Barton upon Humber	37	TA02
Barton-le-Cley	25	TL03
Barvas	64	NB34
Basildon	18	TQ78
Basingstoke	11	SU65
Baslow	31	SK27
Bassenthwaite	44	NY23
Baston	33	TF11
Bath	15	ST76
Bathgate	48	NS96
Batley	35	SE22
Battle	12	TQ71
Baughurst	16	SU56
Baumber	33	TF27
Bawdeswell	27	TG02
Bawtry	36	SK69
Baycliff	38	SD27
Baydon	16	SU27
Beachley	14	ST59
Beaconsfield	17	SU99
Beadnell	49	NU22
Beaminster	9	ST40
Beare Green	11	TQ14
Bearsden	47	NS57
Beattock	43	NT00
Beaulieu	10	SU30
Beauly	60	NH54
Beaumaris	28	SH67
Beaumont	9	JS00
Bebington	29	SJ38
Beccles	27	TM49
Beckenham	17	TQ36
Beckhampton	15	SU06
Beckington	15	ST85
Becquet Vincent	9	JS00
Bedale	40	SE28
Beddgelert	28	SH54
Beddingham	12	TQ40
Bedford	25	TL04
Bedlington	45	NZ28
Bedlinog	14	SO00
Bedwas	14	ST18
Bedworth	24	SP38
Beeford	37	TA15
Beer	8	SY28
Beeston	30	SJ55
Beeston	32	SK53
Beetham	39	SD47
Beetley	27	TF91
Beith	47	NS35
Belbroughton	24	SO97
Belford	49	NU13
Bellingham	44	NY88
Bellochantuy	46	NR63
Bellshill	47	NS76
Belmont	63	HP50
Belmont	34	SD61
Belper	31	SK34
Belsay	45	NZ07
Belton	36	SE70
Bembridge	11	SZ68
Benderloch	54	NM93
Benfleet	12	TQ78
Benllech Bay	28	SH58
Benson	16	SU69
Bentley	36	SE50
Benwick	26	TL39
Bere Alston	5	SX46
Bere Ferrers	5	SX46
Bere Regis	9	SY89
Berkeley Road	15	SO70
Berkeley	15	ST69
Berkhamsted	17	SP90
Bernisdale	58	NG45
Berriedale	67	ND12
Berrow	14	ST25
Berrynarbor	6	SS54
Berwick	12	TQ50
Berwick-upon-Tweed	49	NT95
Bethersden	13	TQ94
Bethesda	28	SH66
Bettyhill	66	NC70
Betws-Y-Coed	29	SH75
Beulah	22	SN95
Beverley	37	TA03
Bewdley	23	SO77
Bexhill-on-Sea	12	TQ70
Bexley	12	TQ47
Bexleyheath	12	TQ47
Bibury	15	SP10
Bicester	16	SP52
Biddenden	13	TQ83
Biddulph	30	SJ85
Bideford	6	SS42
Bidford-on-Avon	24	SP15
Bigbury-on-Sea	5	SX64
Biggar	48	NT03

Biggar	38 SD16	
Biggin Hill	12 TQ45	
Biggleswade	25 TL14	
Bilbrook	7 ST04	
Bilbrough	36 SE54	
Bildeston	19 TL94	
Billericay	18 TQ69	
Billesley	24 SP15	
Billinge	34 SD50	
Billingham	40 NZ42	
Billingshurst	11 TQ02	
Bilston	24 SO99	
Binbrook	37 TF29	
Bingley	35 SE13	
Birchgrove	21 SS79	
Birchington	13 TR36	
Birdlip	24 SO91	
Birdwood	23 SO71	
Birkenhead	34 SJ38	
Birmingham Airport	24 SP18	
Birmingham NEC	24 SP18	
Birmingham	24 SP08	
Birsay	67 HY22	
Birstall	35 SE22	
Bishop Auckland	40 NZ22	
Bishop's Castle	23 SO38	
Bishop's Frome	23 SO64	
Bishop's Lydeard	14 ST12	
Bishop's Stortford	18 TL42	
Bishop's Tawton	6 SS53	
Bishopbriggs	47 NS67	
Bishops Waltham	10 SU51	
Bishopsteignton	8 SX97	
Bishopton	51 NS47	
Blaby	24 SP59	
Black Torrington	6 SS40	
Blackburn	48 NS96	
Blackburn	34 SD62	
Blackeney	27 TG04	
Blackford	52 NN80	
Blackmill	21 SS98	
Blackpool	34 SD33	
Blackrod	34 SD61	
Blackwater	10 SZ58	
Blackwaterfoot	46 NR92	
Blackwell	24 SO97	
Blackwood	14 ST19	
Blaenau Ffestiniog	28 SH74	
Blaenavon	14 SO20	
Blaengarw	21 SS99	
Blagdon	14 ST45	
Blair Atholl	56 NN86	
Blairgowrie	53 NO14	
Blakeney	15 SO60	
Blanchland	45 NY95	
Blandford Forum	9 ST80	
Blawith	38 SD28	
Blaxton	36 SE60	
Blaydon	45 NZ16	
Bleddfa	22 SO26	
Bletchley	25 SP83	
Blickling	27 TG12	
Blisland	5 SX07	
Blockley	24 SP13	
Bloxham	24 SP43	
Blubberhouses	40 SE15	
Blue Anchor	7 ST04	
Blundellsands	38 SD39	
Blyth	45 NZ38	
Blyth	32 SK68	
Blyton	36 SK89	
Bo'ness	48 NT08	
Boat of Garten	56 NH91	
Boddam	63 HU31	
Boddam	63 NK14	
Bodfari	29 SJ06	
Bodinnick	5 SX15	
Bodmin	5 SX06	
Bognor Regis	11 SZ99	
Boldon	45 NZ36	
Bollington	31 SJ97	
Bolney	12 TQ22	
Bolsover	32 SK47	
Bolton Abbey	35 SE05	
Bolton Bridge	35 SE05	
Bolton	34 SD70	
Bolton-le-Sands	39 SD46	
Bomere Heath	30 SJ41	
Bonar Bridge	66 NH69	
Bonawe	55 NN03	
Bonchester Bridge	44 NT51	
Bonnybridge	52 NS88	
Bonnyrigg	48 NT36	
Bontddu	28 SH61	
Bonvilston	14 ST07	
Boot	38 NY10	
Bootle	38 SD18	
Bootle	34 SJ39	
Bordeaux	34 GN00	
Bordon	11 SU73	
Boreham Street	12 TQ61	
Boreham	18 TL70	
Borehamwood	17 TQ19	
Borgue	67 ND12	
Borgue	43 NX64	
Borough Green	12 TQ65	
Boroughbridge	40 SE36	
Borrowdale	38 NY21	
Borth	22 SN68	
Boscastle	5 SX09	
Bosham	11 SU80	
Boston	33 TF34	
Botcheston	24 SK40	
Botesdale	27 TM07	
Bothel	43 NY13	
Bothwell	47 NS75	
Botley	10 SU51	
Bottesford Segebrook	32 SK83	
Bottisham	18 TL56	
Bottom O'th Moor	34 SD71	
Boughton Monchelsea	12 TQ75	
Boughton	13 TR05	
Bouley Bay	9 JS00	
Bourne End	16 SU88	
Bourne	33 TF02	
Bournemouth	10 SZ09	
Bourton-on-the-Water	24 SP12	
Bovey Tracey	8 SX87	
Bovingdon	17 TL00	
Bowdon	30 SJ84	
Bowes	39 NY91	
Bowmore	50 NR35	
Bowness-on-Windermere	39 SD49	
Box	15 ST86	
Bozeat	25 SP95	
Bracklesham Bay	11 SZ89	
Brackley	25 SP53	
Bracknett	16 SU86	
Braco	52 NN80	
Bradford	35 SE13	
Bradford on Avon	15 ST86	
Brading	10 SZ68	
Bradley Stoke	15 ST68	
Bradwell	31 SK18	
Bradwell-on-Sea	19 TM00	
Bradworthy	6 SS31	
Brae	63 HU36	
Braemar	56 NO19	
Braeswick	67 HY63	
Braid Hills	48 NT26	
Braintree	18 TL72	
Braithwaite	38 NY22	
Braithwell	36 SK59	
Bramhall	30 SJ88	
Bramhope	35 SE24	
Bramley	36 SK49	
Brampton	44 NY56	
Brampton	25 TL27	
Brancaster Staithe	26 TF74	
Brancaster	26 TF74	
Brancepeth	45 NZ23	
Brandon	24 SP47	
Brandon	26 TL78	
Brands Hatch	12 TQ56	
Branksome	10 SZ09	
Branston	32 TF06	
Branton	36 SE60	
Bratton Clovelly	5 SX49	
Braunton	6 SS43	
Bray	16 SU98	
Brayford	6 SS63	
Breakish	59 NG62	
Bream	15 SO60	
Brean	14 ST25	
Breasclete	64 NB33	
Brechfa	21 SN53	
Brechin	57 NO56	
Brecon	22 SO02	
Bredon	24 SO93	
Bredwardine	23 SO34	
Brendon	7 SS74	
Brent Knoll	14 ST35	
Brentford	17 TQ17	
Brentwood	18 TQ59	
Brenzett	13 TR02	
Bretby	31 SK22	
Bretton	35 SE21	
Bride	38 NX40	
Bridge of Allan	52 NS78	
Bridge of Balgie	52 NN54	
Bridge of Cally	53 NO15	
Bridge of Don	57 NJ90	
Bridge of Earn	52 NO11	
Bridge of Orchy	55 NN23	
Bridge of Weir	51 NS36	
Bridgend	50 NR36	
Bridgend	21 SS97	
Bridgnorth	23 SO79	
Bridgwater	14 ST33	
Bridlington	41 TA16	
Bridport	9 SY49	
Brierfield	35 SD83	
Brierley Hill	24 SO98	
Brigg	37 TA00	
Brighouse	35 SE12	
Brighstone	10 SZ48	
Brighton	12 TQ30	
Brimington	31 SK47	
Brinklow	24 SP47	
Brinyan	67 HY42	
Brislington	15 ST67	
Bristol Airport	14 ST56	
Bristol	15 ST57	
Briton Ferry	21 SS79	
Brixham	8 SX95	
Broad Haven	20 SM81	
Broadford	58 NG62	
Broadstairs	13 TR36	
Broadway	24 SP03	
Broadwindsor	9 ST40	
Brock	34 SD54	
Brockenhurst	10 SU30	
Brodick	46 NS03	
Bromborough	30 SJ38	
Brome	27 TM17	
Bromham	25 TL05	
Bromley	12 TQ46	
Brompton-on-Swale	40 SE29	
Bromsgrove	24 SO97	
Bromyard	23 SO65	
Brook	10 SU21	
Brooke	27 TM29	
Brookwood	17 SU95	
Broomhill	45 NU20	
Brora	66 NC90	
Brotton	41 NZ61	
Brough	39 NY71	
Broughton Astley	24 SP59	
Broughton	48 NT13	
Broughton	34 SD53	
Broughton	10 SU33	
Broughton-in-Furness	38 SD28	
Broughty Ferry	53 NO43	
Brownhills	31 SK00	
Broxbourne	17 TL30	
Broxburn	48 NT07	
Broxted	18 TL52	
Broxton	30 SJ45	
Bruichladdich	50 NR26	
Bruton	15 ST63	
Bryn	34 SD50	
Brynamman	21 SN71	
Bryneglwys	29 SJ14	
Brynmawr	14 SO11	
Bubwith	36 SE73	
Buchhaven	53 NT39	
Buchlyvie	52 NS59	
Buckden	39 SD97	
Buckden	25 TL16	
Buckhaven	53 NT39	
Buckhurst Hill	18 TQ49	
Buckie	62 NJ46	
Buckingham	25 SP63	
Buckland Newton	9 ST60	
Buckland	24 SP03	
Bucklers Hard	10 SU40	
Buckley	29 SJ26	
Bucklfastleigh	8 SX76	
Bucklow Hill	30 SJ78	
Bucknall	30 SJ84	
Bude	6 SS20	
Budleigh Salterton	8 SY08	
Bugbrooke	25 SP65	
Builth Wells	22 SO05	
Bulkington	24 SP38	
Bulphan	18 TQ68	
Bunessan	54 NM32	
Bungay	27 TM38	
Buntingford	17 TL32	
Bunwell	27 TM19	
Burbage	15 SU26	
Bures	19 TL93	
Burford	16 SP21	
Burgess Hill	12 TQ31	
Burgh by Sands	12 TQ25	
Burgh-by-Sands	44 NY35	
Burghead	61 NJ16	
Burlescombe	7 ST01	
Burley in Wharfdale	35 SE14	
Burley	10 SU20	
Burleydam	30 SJ64	

Burlton................................ 30 SJ42
Burneston........................... 40 SE38
Burnham Deepdale.............. 26 TF84
Burnham Market................. 26 TF84
Burnham............................. 17 SU98
Burnham-on-Crouch............. 19 TQ99
Burnham-on-Sea................. 14 ST34
Burnley.............................. 35 SD83
Burnopfield........................ 45 NZ15
Burnsall............................ 40 SE06
Burnt Yates....................... 40 SE26
Burntisland........................ 48 NT28
Burntwood......................... 31 SK00
Burrafirth.......................... 63 HP61
Burravoe........................... 63 HU57
Burrelton.......................... 52 NO13
Burrington........................... 6 SS61
Burry Port......................... 21 SN40
Burscough Bridge............... 34 SD41
Burscough......................... 34 SD41
Burslem............................ 30 SJ84
Burton Agnes..................... 41 TA16
Burton Bradstock................. 9 SY48
Burton Latimer................... 25 SP97
Burton in Kendal................ 39 SD57
Burton upon Trent.............. 31 SK22
Burton-on-Stather............... 36 SE81
Burwash............................ 12 TQ62
Burwell............................. 18 TL56
Burwick............................ 67 ND48
Bury................................. 35 SD81
Bury St. Edmunds.............. 19 TL86
Bury................................. 11 TQ01
Busby............................... 47 NS55
Bushey.............................. 17 TQ19
Bushley............................. 23 SO83
Butley............................... 19 TM35
Buttermere........................ 38 NY11
Buxton.............................. 31 SK07
Bwlch............................... 22 SO12
Byfleet.............................. 17 TQ06
Byfleet.............................. 17 TQ06
Bylchau............................ 29 SH96

Cadnam............................ 10 SU31
Caeathro........................... 28 SH56
Caergwrle.......................... 29 SJ35
Caerleon........................... 14 ST39
Caernarfon........................ 28 SH46
Caerphilly.......................... 14 ST18
Caersws............................ 22 SO09
Caerwent........................... 14 ST49
Cairndow........................... 51 NN11
Cairnryan.......................... 42 NX06
Caister-on-Sea.................... 27 TG51
Caistor.............................. 37 TA10
Calbourne.......................... 10 SZ48
Caldbeck........................... 44 NY34
Calder Bridge..................... 38 NY00
Calderbrook....................... 35 SD91
Caldercruix........................ 47 NS86
Caldich............................. 51 NN02
Calfsound.......................... 67 HY53
Calgary............................. 54 NM35
Callander.......................... 52 NN60
Callington............................ 5 SX36
Calne................................ 15 ST97
Calvine............................. 56 NN86
Camber............................. 13 TQ91
Camberley......................... 16 SU86
Camborne............................ 4 SW64
Cambridge......................... 15 SO70
Cambridge......................... 18 TL45
Cambusbarron.................... 52 NS79
Cambuslang....................... 47 NS66
Camelford............................ 4 SX08
Campbeltown...................... 46 NR72
Campsea Ash..................... 19 TM35
Candlesby.......................... 33 TF46
Canford Cliffs..................... 10 SZ08
Cannich............................ 60 NH33
Cannock............................ 31 SJ91
Canonbie........................... 44 NY47
Canterbury........................ 13 TR15
Canvey Island.................... 18 TQ78
Caoles.............................. 50 NM04
Capel Curig....................... 28 SH75
Capel Hendre..................... 21 SN51
Capel................................ 11 TQ14
Caputh............................. 52 NO04
Carbis Bay........................... 4 SW53
Carbost............................ 58 NG33
Cardiff.............................. 14 ST17
Cardigan........................... 20 SN14
Cardross........................... 51 NS37
Carfraemill........................ 48 NT55

Carisbrooke....................... 10 SZ48
Cark................................. 39 SD37
Carlisle............................. 44 NY45
Carlops............................. 48 NT15
Carloway........................... 64 NB34
Carlton............................. 40 SE08
Carluke............................. 47 NS85
Carlyon Bay......................... 5 SX05
Carmarthen........................ 21 SN42
Carnforth........................... 39 SD47
Carnoustie......................... 53 NO53
Carnwath........................... 48 NS94
Carperby........................... 40 SE08
Carradale........................... 46 NR83
Carrbridge......................... 61 NH92
Carrefour Selous................... 9 JS00
Carrutherstown................... 43 NY17
Carrville........................... 45 NZ34
Carsphairn........................ 42 NX59
Carstairs........................... 47 NS94
Carter Bar......................... 44 NT60
Carterton.......................... 16 SP20
Cartmel............................ 39 SD37
Castel............................... 38 GN00
Casterton.......................... 39 SD67
Castle Ashby...................... 25 SP85
Castle Bromwich................. 24 SP18
Castle Cary........................ 15 ST63
Castle Combe..................... 15 ST87
Castle Donington................. 31 SK42
Castle Douglas................... 43 NX76
Castle Rising...................... 26 TF62
Castlebay.......................... 64 NL69
Castleford.......................... 36 SE42
Castlemartin....................... 20 SR99
Castleside......................... 45 NZ04
Castleton.......................... 41 NZ60
Castleton.......................... 31 SK18
Castleton.......................... 14 ST28
Castletown........................ 38 SC26
Castletown........................ 67 ND16
Castletown........................ 38 SC26
Caterham........................... 12 TQ35
Catterick Bridge................. 40 SE29
Catterick Garrison.............. 40 SE19
Cautley............................. 39 SD69
Cavendish.......................... 18 TL84
Caversham......................... 16 SU77
Cawdor............................. 61 NH85
Cawood............................. 36 SE53
Caxton.............................. 18 TL35
Cemaes Bay....................... 28 SH39
Cemmaes Road................... 22 SH80
Cerne Abbas........................ 9 ST60
Cerrigydrudion.................... 29 SH94
Chacewater.......................... 4 SW74
Chaddesley Corbett.............. 23 SO87
Chadlington....................... 16 SP32
Chadwell Heath.................. 12 TQ48
Chagford............................. 8 SX78
Chale............................... 10 SZ47
Chale............................... 10 SZ47
Chalfont St Peter................ 17 TQ09
Chalford............................ 15 SO80
Chalgrove.......................... 16 SU69
Challock............................ 13 TR05
Chandler's Ford.................. 10 SU42
Chapel St Leonards............. 33 TF57
Chapel-en-le-Frith.............. 31 SK08
Chapelton.......................... 47 NS64
Chapeltown........................ 36 SK39
Chard.................................. 8 ST30
Chardstock........................... 8 ST30
Charing............................. 13 TQ94
Charingworth..................... 24 SP13
Charlbury.......................... 16 SP31
Charlecote......................... 24 SP25
Charlesworth...................... 35 SK09
Charlton Marshall................. 9 ST80
Charlwood......................... 11 TQ24
Charmouth........................... 9 SY39
Charnock Richard............... 34 SD51
Chatburn........................... 35 SD74
Chatham............................ 12 TQ76
Chattenden........................ 12 TQ77
Chatteris........................... 26 TL38
Chatton............................. 49 NU02
Chawleigh............................ 6 SS71
Cheadle Hulme.................... 30 SJ88
Cheadle............................. 35 SJ88
Cheadle............................. 31 SK04
Cheam.............................. 12 TQ26
Cheddar............................ 14 ST45
Chelford............................ 30 SJ87
Chelmsford........................ 18 TL70
Chelsfield.......................... 12 TQ46
Cheltenham........................ 24 SO92

Chelwood Gate................... 12 TQ43
Chelwood.......................... 15 ST66
Chenies............................ 17 TQ09
Chepstow.......................... 14 ST59
Cheriton Bishop.................... 8 SX79
Cheriton Fitzpaine................. 7 SS80
Chertsey........................... 17 TQ06
Chesham........................... 17 SP90
Cheshunt........................... 17 TL30
Chessington....................... 17 TQ16
Chester............................. 30 SJ46
Chester-le-Street................ 45 NZ25
Chesterfield....................... 31 SK37
Chesterton......................... 30 SJ84
Chichester......................... 11 SU80
Chiddingfold...................... 11 SU93
Chigwell............................ 18 TQ49
Chilcompton....................... 15 ST65
Chillington........................... 8 SX74
Chilmark........................... 15 ST93
Chilwell............................ 32 SK53
Chingford.......................... 18 TQ39
Chinnor............................. 16 SP70
Chippenham....................... 15 ST97
Chipperfield....................... 17 TL00
Chipping Campden.............. 24 SP13
Chipping Norton................. 24 SP32
Chipping............................ 34 SD64
Chirbury............................ 23 SO29
Chirk................................ 29 SJ23
Chirnside.......................... 49 NT85
Chiseldon.......................... 15 SU17
Chislehurst........................ 12 TQ47
Chittlehamholt...................... 6 SS62
Chobham........................... 17 SU96
Chollerford........................ 45 NY97
Chorley............................. 34 SD51
Chorleywood...................... 17 TQ09
Chorlton............................ 30 SJ44
Christchurch....................... 23 SO51
Christchurch....................... 10 SZ19
Chudleigh Knighton............... 8 SX87
Chudleigh............................ 8 SX87
Chulmleigh........................... 6 SS61
Church Stoke...................... 23 SO29
Church Stretton.................. 23 SO49
Churston Ferrers................... 8 SX95
Churt................................ 11 SU83
Cilgerran........................... 20 SN14
Cinderford......................... 23 SO61
Cirencester........................ 15 SP00
Clachan............................ 46 NR75
Clachan-Seil...................... 51 NM71
Clacton-on-Sea................... 19 TM11
Cladich............................. 51 NN02
Clanfield........................... 16 SP20
Clanfield........................... 11 SU71
Claonaig........................... 46 NR85
Clapham............................ 39 SD76
Clapham............................ 25 TL05
Clarach............................. 22 SM68
Clare................................ 18 TL74
Clavering........................... 18 TL43
Clawton.............................. 6 SX39
Clayton-le-Moors................ 35 SD73
Clayworth.......................... 36 SK78
Clearwell.......................... 14 SO50
Cleator Moor...................... 38 NY01
Cleckheaton....................... 35 SE12
Cleethorpes........................ 37 TA30
Cleeve Hill........................ 24 SO92
Cleeve.............................. 14 ST46
Cleish.............................. 56 NO09
Cleland............................. 47 NS75
Cleobury Mortimer.............. 23 SO67
Cleobury North................... 23 SO68
Clevedon........................... 14 ST47
Cleveleys.......................... 34 SD34
Cley next the Sea................ 27 TG04
Cliffe................................ 12 TQ77
Clifton.............................. 34 SD43
Cliftonville......................... 13 TR37
Climping........................... 11 TQ00
Clitheroe........................... 35 SD74
Clophill............................. 25 TL03
Cloughton.......................... 41 TA09
Clova............................... 57 NO37
Clovelly.............................. 6 SS32
Clowne............................. 32 SK47
Clun................................. 23 SO28
Clydebank......................... 47 NS47
Clynder............................. 51 NS28
Clynnogfawr....................... 28 SH44
Clyro............................... 22 SO24
Clyst Honiton....................... 8 SX99
Coalville............................ 31 SK41
Coatbridge......................... 47 NS76

Cobham	17	TQ16
Cobridge	30	SJ84
Cockburnspath	49	NT77
Cockenzie	48	NT47
Cockermouth	43	NY13
Coddenham	19	TM15
Codicote	17	TL21
Codnor	31	SK44
Codsall	23	SJ80
Coggeshall	19	TL82
Colby	38	SC27
Colchester	19	TL92
Coldingham	49	NT96
Coleford	15	SO51
Colerne	15	ST87
Coleshill	24	SP28
Colinton	48	NT26
Colintraive	51	NS07
Collieston	63	NK12
Collin	43	NY07
Collingham	36	SE34
Collington	23	SO66
Colnbrook	17	TQ07
Colne	35	SD84
Colsterworth	32	SK92
Coltishall	27	TG21
Colvend	43	NX85
Colwich	31	SK02
Colwyn Bay	29	SH87
Colyton	8	SY29
Combe Martin	6	SS54
Combeinteignhead	8	SX97
Comrie	52	NN72
Congleton	30	SJ86
Congresbury	14	ST46
Coningsby	33	TF25
Conington	25	TL18
Conisbrough	36	SK59
Coniston	38	SD39
Connah's Quay	29	SJ26
Connel	54	NM93
Conon Bridge	60	NH55
Consett	45	NZ15
Constantine Bay	4	SW87
Contin	60	NH45
Conwy	29	SH77
Cooden Beach	12	TQ70
Cookham	16	SU88
Copplestone	7	SS70
Copthorne	12	TQ33
Corbiere	9	JS00
Corbridge	45	NY96
Corby Glen	32	TF02
Corby	25	SP88
Corfe Castle	9	SY98
Corfe Mullen	10	SY99
Corgarff	57	NJ20
Corhampton	10	SU62
Corley Ash	24	SP28
Cornhill	62	NJ55
Cornhill-on-Tweed	49	NT83
Cornwood	5	SX65
Corpach	55	NN07
Corran	59	NG80
Corrie	46	NS04
Corris	28	SH70
Corse Lawn	23	SO83
Corsham	15	ST87
Corsley	15	ST84
Corstorphine	48	NT17
Corton	27	TM59
Corwen	29	SJ04
Coryton	12	TQ78
Cosham	11	SU60
Coshieville	52	NN74
Cossington	32	SK61
Cottenham	18	TL46
Cottered	18	TL32
Cottesmore	32	SK91
Cottingham	25	SP89
Coulport	51	NS28
Coulsdon	12	TQ35
Coundon	40	NZ22
Coupar Angus	53	NO23
Cove	64	NG89
Cove	51	NS28
Coventry	24	SP37
Coverack	4	SW71
Cowbridge	14	SS97
Cowdenbeath	53	NT19
Cowes	10	SZ49
Cowfold	11	TQ22
Cowley	17	TQ08
Coxhoe	45	NZ33
Coxwold	40	SE57
Coylumbridge	56	NH91
Coylton	47	NS41
Crackington Haven	6	SX19
Cradley Heath	24	SO98
Cragg	35	SE02
Craigellachie	61	NJ24
Craighouse	50	NR56
Craignure	54	NM73
Craigrothie	53	NO31
Crail	53	NO60
Cramlington	45	NZ27
Cramond Foreshore	48	NT27
Cranborne	10	SU01
Cranbrook	12	TQ73
Cranfield	25	SP94
Cranleigh	11	TQ03
Crantock	4	SW76
Cranwell	33	TF04
Crapstone	5	SX56
Crathorne	40	NZ40
Craven Arms	23	SO48
Crawford	48	NS92
Crawfordjohn	47	NS82
Crawley	12	TQ23
Crayford	12	TQ57
Creagorry	64	NF74
Crediton	7	SS80
Creetown	42	NX45
Cregneish	38	SC16
Cressage	23	SJ50
Crewe	30	SJ75
Crewkerne	9	ST40
Crianlarich	55	NN32
Criccieth	28	SH53
Crick	25	SP57
Crickhowell	22	SO21
Cricklade	15	SU09
Crieff	52	NN82
Crinan	51	NR79
Crockernwell	8	SX79
Crocketford	43	NX87
Croft-on-Tees	40	NZ20
Cromarty	61	NH76
Cromdale	61	NJ02
Cromer	27	TG24
Cronton	34	SJ48
Crook	45	NZ13
Crookham Village	11	SU75
Crooklands	39	SD58
Crosby	38	SC37
Crosby	34	SJ39
Crosby-on-Eden	44	NY45
Cross Hands	21	SN51
Cross-in-Hand	12	TQ52
Crossmichael	43	NX76
Crossway Green	23	SO86
Crosthwaite	39	SD49
Croston	34	SD41
Croughton	24	SP53
Crowborough	12	TQ53
Crowfield	19	TM15
Crowland	33	TF21
Crowle	36	SE71
Crowthorne	16	SU86
Croy	61	NH74
Croyde	6	SS43
Croydon	17	TQ36
Cruden Bay	63	NK03
Cruden Bay	63	NK13
Crudgington	30	SJ61
Crudwell	15	ST99
Crugybar	21	SN63
Crumlin	14	ST29
Cuckfield	12	TQ32
Cuckney	32	SK57
Cuddington	30	SJ57
Cudworth	36	SE30
Cuffley	17	TL30
Culcheth	34	SJ69
Cullen	62	NJ56
Cullercoats	45	NZ37
Cullingworth	35	SE03
Cullivoe	63	HP50
Cullompton	7	ST00
Culmstock	7	ST11
Culnacnoc	58	NG57
Culross	48	NS98
Cumbernauld	47	NS77
Cuminestown	62	NJ75
Cummingston	61	NJ16
Cumnock	47	NS51
Cumrew	44	NY55
Cupar	53	NO31
Cwm Ystwyth	22	SN77
Cwm-y-Glo	28	SH56
Cwmbran	14	ST29
Cymmer	21	SS89
Cynwyl Elfed	21	SN32
Dagenham	18	TQ58
Dailly	42	NS20
Dairy	47	NS24
Dalbeattie	43	NX86
Dale	20	SM80
Dalgety Bay	48	NT18
Dalkeith	48	NT36
Dallas	61	NJ15
Dalmally	55	NN12
Dalmellington	47	NS40
Dalry	43	NX68
Dalrymple	47	NS31
Dalston	44	NY35
Dalton	43	NY17
Dalwhinnie	56	NN68
Daresbury	30	SJ58
Darlaston	24	SO99
Darley Dale	31	SK26
Darlington	40	NZ21
Darrington	36	SE41
Dartford	12	TQ57
Dartmeet	5	SX67
Dartmouth	8	SX85
Darton	35	SE31
Darvel	47	NS53
Darwen	34	SD62
Datchet	17	SU97
Davenham	30	SJ67
Daventry	25	SP56
Daviot	60	NH73
Dawley	30	SJ60
Dawlish	8	SX97
Deal	13	TR35
Deanston	52	NN60
Debenham	19	TM16
Deddington	24	SP43
Dedham	19	TM03
Deepcut	16	SU95
Deeping St James	33	TF10
Deeping St Nicholas	33	TF21
Deganwy	29	SH77
Delabole	5	SX08
Delph	35	SD90
Denaby	36	SK49
Denbigh	29	SJ06
Denby Dale	35	SE20
Denham	17	TQ08
Denholm	48	NT51
Denholme	35	SE03
Dennington	19	TM26
Denny	52	NS88
Denshaw	35	SD91
Dent	39	SD78
Denton	35	SJ99
Derby	31	SK33
Derbyhaven	38	SC26
Dervaig	54	NM45
Desborough	25	SP88
Desford	24	SK40
Detling	12	TQ75
Devil's Bridge	22	SN77
Devises	15	SU06
Dewsbury	35	SE22
Dhoon	38	SC48
Diabaig	59	NG75
Dibden Purlieu	10	SU40
Didcot	16	SU58
Dinas Mawddwy	29	SH81
Dingwall	60	NH55
Dinnet	57	NO49
Dinnington	32	SK58
Dippen	46	NR73
Dirleton	48	NT58
Diseworth	31	SK42
Disley	31	SJ98
Diss	27	TM17
Ditchling	12	TQ31
Ditton Priors	23	SO68
Dobwalls	5	SX26
Docking	26	TF73
Doddington	49	NT93
Doddington	26	TL39
Doddington	13	TQ95
Dodworth	35	SE30
Dogmersfield	16	SU75
Dolfor	22	SO18
Dolgellau	28	SH71
Dollar	52	NS99
Dolphinton	48	NT14
Dolwyddelan	28	SH75
Doncaster	36	SE50
Donington	33	TF23
Donnington	23	SJ60
Dorchester	9	SY69
Dorchester-on-Thames	16	SU59
Dores	60	NH53
Dorking	11	TQ14

Dormington ... 23 SO54
Dornie ... 59 NG82
Dornoch ... 61 NH78
Dorridge ... 24 SP17
Douglas ... 38 SC37
Douglas ... 47 NS83
Douglas ... 38 SC37
Dounby ... 67 HY22
Doune ... 52 NN70
Dover ... 13 TR34
Dovercourt ... 19 TM23
Down Thomas ... 5 SX55
Downderry ... 5 SX35
Downton ... 10 SU12
Drakemyre ... 47 NS25
Draycott ... 31 SK43
Drimnin ... 54 NM55
Droitwich ... 23 SO86
Dronfield ... 31 SK37
Droxford ... 10 SU61
Drumbeg ... 65 NC13
Drumclog ... 47 NS63
Drummore ... 42 NX13
Drumnadrochit ... 60 NH53
Drybrook ... 23 SO61
Drymen ... 52 NS48
Duddington ... 25 SK90
Dudley ... 24 SO99
Duffield ... 31 SK34
Dufftown ... 61 NJ33
Duirinish ... 59 NG73
Dulnain Bridge ... 61 NH92
Dulverton ... 7 SS92
Dumbarton ... 51 NS37
Dumfries ... 43 NX97
Dunbar ... 49 NT67
Dunbeath ... 67 ND12
Dunblane ... 52 NN70
Dunchurch ... 24 SP47
Dundee ... 53 NO43
Dundonnell ... 59 NH08
Dundry ... 15 ST56
Dunfermline ... 52 NT08
Dunholme ... 32 TF07
Dunkeld ... 52 NO04
Dunkirk ... 13 TR05
Dunnet ... 67 ND27
Dunning ... 52 NO01
Dunoon ... 51 NS17
Dunragit ... 42 NX15
Duns ... 49 NT75
Dunscore ... 43 NX88
Dunsfold ... 11 TQ03
Dunsop Bridge ... 34 SD64
Dunstable ... 17 TL02
Dunster ... 7 SS94
Dunton Bassett ... 24 SP59
Dunton Green ... 12 TQ55
Duntulm ... 58 NG47
Dunvegan ... 58 NG24
Dunwich ... 27 TM47
Durham ... 45 NZ24
Durness ... 65 NC46
Duror ... 55 NM95
Dursley ... 15 ST79
Duxford ... 18 TL44
Dyce ... 57 NJ81
Dyffryn Ardudwy ... 28 SH52
Dylife ... 22 SN89
Dymchurch ... 13 TR12
Dysart ... 53 NT39
Dyserth ... 29 SJ07

Eaglescliffe ... 40 NZ41
Eaglesfield ... 44 NY27
Eaglesham ... 47 NS55
Ealing ... 17 TQ18
Eamont Bridge ... 39 NY52
Earby ... 35 SD94
Earl Barton ... 25 SP86
Earl Shilton ... 24 SP49
Earlston ... 48 NT53
Earsdon ... 45 NZ27
Easdale ... 50 NM71
Easington ... 45 NZ44
Easington ... 41 NZ71
Easington ... 37 TA41
Easingwold ... 40 SE56
East Bilney ... 27 TF91
East Challow ... 16 SU38
East Cowes ... 10 SZ59
East Croachy ... 60 NH62
East Dereham ... 27 TF91
East Grinstead ... 12 TQ33
East Harling ... 27 TL98
East Horndon ... 18 TQ68

East Horsley ... 11 TQ05
East Kilbride ... 47 NS65
East Leake ... 32 SK52
East Linton ... 48 NT57
East Lulworth ... 9 SY88
East Nilney ... 26 TF91
East Peckham ... 12 TQ64
East Portlemouth ... 8 SX73
East Preston ... 11 TQ00
East Retford ... 32 SK78
East Rudham ... 26 TF82
East Wittering ... 11 SZ79
Eastbourne ... 12 TV69
Eastchurch ... 13 TQ97
Eastdean ... 12 TV59
Easter Skeld ... 63 HU34
Eastfield ... 41 TA08
Eastham ... 30 SJ38
Eastleigh ... 10 SU41
Eastwood ... 31 SK44
Eathorpe ... 24 SP36
Ebbw Vale ... 14 SO10
Ebchester ... 45 NZ15
Ecclefechan ... 43 NY17
Eccles ... 49 NT74
Eccles ... 35 SJ79
Ecclesfield ... 36 SK39
Eccleshall ... 30 SJ82
Echt ... 57 NJ70
Edderton ... 60 NH78
Edenbridge ... 12 TQ44
Edenhall ... 44 NY53
Edgeware ... 17 TQ19
Edinbane ... 58 NG35
Edinburgh Airport ... 48 NT17
Edinburgh ... 48 NT27
Edmonton ... 17 TQ39
Edmundbyers ... 45 NZ05
Edwinstowe ... 32 SK66
Edzell ... 57 NO56
Egerton ... 34 SD71
Eggesford ... 6 SS61
Egginton ... 24 SP22
Egglescliffe ... 40 NZ41
Egglestone ... 39 NY92
Egham ... 17 TQ07
Eglingham ... 49 NU11
Eglwysfach ... 22 SN69
Eglwyswrw ... 20 SN13
Egremont ... 38 NY01
Egton ... 41 NZ80
Elan ... 22 SN96
Elberton ... 15 ST68
Elcot ... 16 SU36
Elderslie ... 51 NS46
Elgin ... 61 NJ26
Elgol ... 58 NG51
Elie ... 53 NO40
Elland ... 35 SE12
Ellesmere Port ... 30 SJ47
Ellesmere ... 30 SJ43
Ellingham ... 27 TM39
Ellon ... 63 NJ93
Elmstead Market ... 19 TM02
Elsdon ... 45 NY99
Elstree ... 17 TQ19
Elterwater ... 39 NY30
Eltisley ... 18 TL25
Elton ... 25 TL09
Elveden ... 26 TL88
Elvington ... 36 SE64
Elwick ... 45 NZ43
Ely ... 26 TL58
Embleton ... 49 NU22
Embo ... 66 NH89
Emborough ... 15 ST65
Emsworth ... 11 SU70
Endon ... 31 SJ95
Enfield ... 17 TQ39
Ennerdale Bridge ... 38 NY01
Entercommon ... 40 NZ30
Epping ... 18 TL40
Epsom ... 17 TQ26
Erdington ... 24 SP19
Eriboll ... 65 NC45
Eriska ... 54 NM94
Erith ... 12 TQ57
Ermington ... 5 SX65
Errogie ... 60 NH52
Erskine ... 47 NS47
Ervie ... 42 NW96
Erwood ... 22 SO04
Esher ... 17 TQ16
Eskdale Green ... 38 NY10
Eskdalemuir ... 44 NY29
Ettington ... 24 SP24
Ettrickbridge ... 48 NT32

Evanton ... 60 NH56
Evercreech ... 15 ST63
Evershot ... 9 ST50
Eversley ... 16 SU76
Evesham ... 24 SP04
Ewell ... 17 TQ26
Ewen ... 15 SU09
Ewhurst ... 11 TQ04
Ewloe ... 29 SJ26
Ewyas Harrold ... 23 SO32
Exbourne ... 6 SS60
Exebridge ... 7 SS92
Exeter ... 8 SX99
Exford ... 7 SS83
Exmouth ... 8 SY08
Eye ... 25 TF20
Eye ... 27 TM17
Eyemouth ... 49 NT96
Eynsgam ... 16 SP40

Fairbourne ... 28 SH61
Fairford ... 15 SP10
Fairlie ... 46 NS25
Fairy Cross ... 6 SS42
Fakenham ... 26 TF93
Faldingworth ... 33 TF08
Falfield ... 15 ST69
Falkirk ... 52 NS87
Falkland ... 53 NO20
Falmouth ... 4 SW83
Far Sawrey ... 39 SD39
Fareham ... 10 SU50
Faringdon ... 15 SU29
Farington ... 10 SU60
Farnborough ... 16 SU85
Farnham Common ... 17 SU98
Farnham ... 11 SU84
Farningham ... 12 TQ56
Farnworth ... 35 SD70
Faringdon ... 16 SU29
Farrington Gurney ... 15 ST65
Farthing Corner ... 12 TQ86
Faugh ... 44 NY55
Faversham ... 13 TR06
Fawley ... 10 SU40
Fazeley ... 24 SK20
Fearnan ... 52 NN74
Felixstowe ... 19 TM23
Felling ... 45 NZ26
Feltham ... 17 TQ17
Felton ... 45 NU10
Feltwell ... 26 TL79
Fenny Bentley ... 31 SK14
Fenny Bridges ... 8 SY19
Fenny Compton ... 24 SP45
Fenny Drayton ... 24 SP39
Fenstanton ... 18 TL36
Fenwick ... 47 NS44
Feock ... 4 SW83
Fermain Bay ... 4 GN00
Ferndown ... 10 SU00
Ferness ... 61 NH94
Ferrybridge S A ... 36 SE42
Ferryhill ... 45 NZ23
Fettercairn ... 57 NO67
Ffestiniog ... 28 SH74
Filey ... 41 TA18
Fillongley ... 24 SP28
Finchingfield ... 18 TL63
Finchley ... 17 TQ29
Findhorn ... 61 NJ06
Findochty ... 62 NJ46
Findon ... 11 TQ10
Finedon ... 25 SP97
Finningham ... 19 TM06
Finstown ... 67 HY31
Fintry ... 52 NS68
Fionnphort ... 54 NM32
Fir Tree ... 45 NZ13
Firth ... 60 NH76
Fishbourne ... 10 SZ59
Fishguard ... 20 SM93
Fittleworth ... 11 TQ01
Five Oaks ... 9 JS00
Five Oaks ... 11 TQ02
Fivehead ... 14 ST32
Flamborough ... 41 TA27
Flax Bourton ... 14 ST56
Fleet ... 16 SU85
Fleetwood ... 34 SD34
Flimby ... 43 NY03
Flimwell ... 12 TQ73
Flint ... 29 SJ27
Flitwick ... 17 TL03
Flockton ... 35 SE21
Flodigarry ... 58 NG47

Flore	25	SP66
Fochabers	61	NJ35
Folkestone	13	TR23
Folly Gate	6	SX59
Fontmell Magna	9	ST81
Fontwell	11	SU90
Ford	51	NM80
Ford	15	ST87
Forden	23	SJ20
Fordingbridge	10	SU11
Fordoun	57	NO77
Fordwich	13	TR15
Forest Row	12	TQ43
Forfar	53	NO45
Formby	34	SD30
Forres	61	NJ05
Forsinard	66	NC84
Fort Augustus	60	NH30
Fort William	55	NN17
Forteviot	52	NO01
Forth	47	NS95
Fortingall	52	NN74
Forton S A	39	SD45
Forton	34	SD45
Fortrose	60	NH75
Fossebridge	15	SP01
Four Marks	11	SU63
Four Mile Bridge	28	SH27
Fourwinds	5	SX17
Fowey	5	SX15
Fownhope	23	SO53
Foyers	60	NH42
Fraddam	4	SW53
Fraddon	4	SW95
Fradley	31	SK11
Framlingham	19	TM26
Frampton Cotterell	15	ST68
Framwellgate Moor	45	NZ24
Fraserburgh	63	NJ96
Freckenham	26	TL67
Freckleton	34	SD42
Freshford	15	ST76
Freshwater	10	SZ38
Freswick	67	ND36
Freuchie	53	NO20
Fridaythorpe	41	SE85
Frimley	16	SU85
Frinton-on-Sea	19	TM21
Friockheim	53	NO54
Friskney	33	TF45
Frizington	38	NY01
Frodsham	30	SJ57
Frome	15	ST74
Froncyllte	29	SJ24
Fulletby	33	TF27
Furnace	51	NN00
Furnace	51	NS09
Fyfield	16	SU49
Fyvie	62	NJ73
Gailey	30	SJ91
Gainsborough	36	SK88
Gairloch	59	NG87
Gairlochy	55	NN18
Galashiels	48	NT43
Galgate	39	SD45
Galston	47	NS43
Gamlingay	18	TL25
Ganllwyd	28	SH72
Garboldisham	27	TM08
Garelochhead	51	NS29
Garforth	36	SE43
Gargrave	35	SD95
Garlieston	42	NX44
Garlogie	57	NJ70
Garn Dolbenmaen	28	SH44
Garnant	21	SN61
Garrigill	44	NY74
Garstang	34	SD44
Garth	22	SN94
Garthmyl	22	SO19
Garve	60	NH36
Gatehouse of Fleet	43	NX55
Gateshead	45	NZ26
Gatwick	12	TQ24
Gaydon	24	SP35
Gedney Drove End	33	TF42
Gerrards Cross	17	TQ08
Giffnock	47	NS55
Gifford	48	NT56
Gigha Island	46	NR64
Gillan	4	SW72
Gillingham	15	ST82
Gillingham	12	TQ76
Gilmerton	52	NN82
Gilmerton	48	NT26
Gilwern	23	SO21
Girvan	42	NX19
Gisburn	35	SD84
Gittisham	8	SY19
Glamis	53	NO34
Glanton	49	NU01
Glapwell	32	SK46
Glasbury	22	SO13
Glasgow Airport	51	NS46
Glasgow	47	NS56
Glastonbury	14	ST53
Glenbarr	46	NR63
Glenborrodale	54	NM66
Glenbrittle	58	NG42
Glencaple	43	NX96
Glencarse	53	NO12
Glencoe	55	NN15
Gleneagles	52	NN90
Gleneig	59	NG81
Glenfarg	53	NO11
Glenfinnan	54	NM98
Glenkindie	57	NJ41
Glenlivet	61	NJ12
Glenluce	42	NX15
Glenmaye	38	SC27
Glenridding	39	NY31
Glenrothes	53	NO20
Glenshee	56	NO16
Glenshiel	59	NG91
Glossop	35	SK09
Gloucester	23	SO81
Glyn Ceiriog	29	SJ23
Glyn Neath	21	SN80
Glyncorrwg	21	SS89
Goathland	41	NZ80
Gobowen	29	SJ33
Godalming	11	SU94
Godmanchester	25	TL27
Godshill	10	SZ58
Godstone	12	TQ35
Golant	5	SX15
Golspie	66	NH89
Goodrich	23	SO51
Goodrington	8	SX86
Goodwick	20	SM93
Goodwood	11	SU81
Goole	36	SE72
Gordon	49	NT64
Gorey	9	JS00
Goring	16	SU68
Goring-by-Sea	11	TQ10
Gorleston on Sea	27	TG50
Gorseinon	21	SS59
Gosberton	33	TF23
Gosforth	38	NY00
Gosforth	45	NZ26
Gosport	10	SZ69
Goudhurst	12	TQ73
Gowerton	21	SS59
Grain	13	TQ87
Gramisdale	64	NF85
Grandes Rocques	9	GN00
Grands Chemins	9	JS00
Grandtully	52	NN95
Grange	38	NY21
Grange-over-Sands	39	SD47
Grangemouth	52	NS98
Grangetown	40	NZ52
Grantham	32	SK93
Grantown-on-Spey	61	NJ02
Grantshouse	49	NT86
Grasmere	39	NY30
Grassington	40	SE06
Graveley	18	TL22
Gravesend	12	TQ67
Grays	12	TQ67
Great Asby	39	NY61
Great Ayton	40	NZ51
Great Barr	24	SP09
Great Bedwyn	16	SU26
Great Bentley	19	TM12
Great Bircham	26	TF73
Great Blakenham	19	TM15
Great Bridgeford	30	SJ82
Great Chesterford	18	TL54
Great Cumbrae	46	NS15
Great Driffield	41	TA05
Great Dunmow	18	TL62
Great Gidding	25	TL18
Great Glen	25	SP69
Great Haywood	31	SJ92
Great Kimble	16	SP80
Great Langdale	38	NY30
Great Leighs	18	TL71
Great Milton	16	SP60
Great Missenden	16	SP80
Great Ponton	32	SK93
Great Shelford	18	TL45
Great Staughton	25	TL16
Great Torrington	6	SS41
Great Wakering	19	TQ98
Great Witchingham	27	TG01
Great Witley	23	SO76
Great Yarmouth	27	TG50
Great Yeldham	18	TL73
Greatstone-on-Sea	13	TR02
Green Hammerton	40	SE45
Greenfield	35	SD90
Greenfield	29	SJ17
Greenford	17	TQ18
Greenhead	44	NY66
Greenlaw	49	NT74
Greenloaning	52	NN80
Greenock	51	NS27
Greetland	35	SE02
Greta Bridge	40	NZ01
Gretna Green	44	NY36
Gretna	44	NY36
Greystoke	44	NY43
Grimoldby	37	TF38
Grimsargh	34	SD53
Grimsby	37	TA20
Grimston	26	TF72
Grindleford	31	SK27
Gringley-on-the-Hill	36	SK79
Grizedale	39	SD39
Groby	32	SK50
Groeslon	28	SH45
Gronant	29	SJ08
Grosmont	41	NZ80
Grouville Bay	9	JS00
Guard Bridge	53	NO41
Guildford	11	SU94
Guilsborough	25	SP67
Guilsfield	29	SJ21
Guisborough	40	NZ61
Guiseley	35	SE14
Guist	27	TF92
Gullane	48	NT48
Gunnerside	39	SD99
Gunnislake	5	SX47
Gunthorpe	32	SK64
Gurnard	10	SZ49
Gutcher	63	HU59
Guthrie	53	NO55
Guyhirn	26	TF30
Gwbert-on-Sea	20	SN14
Gweek	4	SW72
Gwernymynydd	29	SJ26
Gwithian	4	SW54
Hackness	41	SE99
Haddenham	16	SP70
Haddenham	26	TL47
Haddington	48	NT57
Haddiscoe	27	TM49
Hadleigh	19	TM04
Hadleigh	18	TQ88
Hadley Wood	17	TQ29
Hadlow	12	TQ64
Hailsham	12	TQ50
Hainault	18	TQ49
Halesowen	24	SO98
Halesworth	27	TM37
Halifax	35	SE02
Halkirk	67	ND15
Halkyn	29	SJ17
Halland	12	TQ41
Hallworthy	5	SX18
Halstead	18	TL83
Halwell	8	SX75
Halwill Junction	6	SS40
Ham Street	13	TR03
Hamble	10	SU40
Hambleton	36	SE53
Hamilton	47	NS75
Hamnavoe	63	HU33
Hampson Green	34	SD55
Hampstead Norreys	16	SU57
Hampsthwaite	40	SE25
Hampton	17	TQ16
Hampton in Arden	24	SP28
Hanchurch	30	SJ84
Handcross	12	TQ22
Handforth	30	SJ88
Handley	30	SJ45
Handsacre	31	SK01
Handsworth	24	SP08
Hanford	30	SJ84
Hankerton	15	ST99
Hanley	30	SJ84
Hanslope	25	SP84
Happisburgh	27	TG33

Harbertonford	8	SX75
Harborne	24	SP08
Hare Street	18	TL32
Harewood	35	SE34
Harlech	28	SH53
Harleston	27	TM28
Harlosh	58	NG24
Harlow	18	TL41
Harlyn Bay	4	SW87
Harmondsworth	17	TQ07
Harold Wood	18	TQ59
Haroldswick	63	HP61
Harome	40	SE68
Harpenden	17	TL11
Harrogate	35	SE35
Harrold	25	SP95
Harrow	17	TQ18
Harrow Weald	17	TQ19
Hartfield	12	TQ43
Hartford	30	SJ67
Harthill	47	NS96
Hartington	31	SK16
Hartland	6	SS22
Hartlepool	45	NZ53
Hartley Wintney	16	SU75
Harvington	24	SP04
Harwich	19	TM23
Haslemere	11	SU93
Haslingden	35	SD72
Hassocks	12	TQ21
Hastings	12	TQ80
Hatch Beauchamp	8	ST32
Hatfield Heath	18	TL51
Hatfield	36	SE60
Hatfield	17	TL20
Hatherleigh	6	SS50
Hathern	32	SK52
Hathersage	31	SK28
Hatt	5	SX36
Hatton	63	NK03
Haughton-le-Skerne	40	NZ31
Hautes Croix	9	JS00
Havant	11	SU70
Haven St.	10	SZ59
Haverfordwest	20	SM91
Haverhill	18	TL64
Hawarden	29	SJ36
Hawes	39	SD88
Haweswater	39	NY41
Hawick	48	NT51
Hawkchurch	9	ST30
Hawkhurst	12	TQ73
Hawkinge	13	TR24
Hawkridge	7	SS83
Hawkshead	39	SD39
Hawnby	40	SE58
Haworth	35	SE03
Haxby	40	SE65
Hay-on-Wye	23	SO24
Haydock	34	SJ59
Haydon Bridge	44	NY86
Hayes	17	TQ08
Hayle	4	SW53
Hayling Island	11	SU70
Hayton	44	NY55
Haytor	8	SX77
Haywards Heath	12	TQ32
Hazel Grove	30	SJ98
Heacham	26	TF63
Headcorn	13	TQ84
Headingley	35	SE23
Heanor	31	SK44
Heathfield	12	TQ52
Heathrow Airport	17	TQ07
Hebburn	45	NZ36
Hebden Bridge	35	SD92
Heckington	33	TF14
Hedge End	10	SU41
Hednesford	31	SK01
Hedon	37	TA12
Heighington	40	NZ22
Helensburgh	51	NS28
Helford	4	SW72
Hellifield	39	SD85
Helmingham	19	TM15
Helmsdale	67	ND01
Helmsley	40	SE68
Helpringham	33	TF14
Helsby	30	SJ47
Helston	4	SW62
Hemel Hempstead	17	TL00
Hemingford Abbots	26	TL27
Hempnall	27	TM29
Hempsted	23	SO81
Hemsby	27	TG41
Hemsworth	36	SE41
Hemyock	7	ST11
Henfield	11	TQ21
Henlade	14	ST22
Henley	19	TM15
Henley on Thames	16	SU78
Henley-in-Arden	24	SP16
Henllan	29	SJ06
Henlow	25	TL13
Henstridge	15	ST72
Hereford	23	SO54
Hermitage	16	SU57
Herne Bay	13	TR16
Hertford Heath	17	TL31
Hertford	17	TL31
Hesketh Bank	34	SD42
Hesleden	45	NZ43
Hessle	37	TA02
Heswall	29	SJ28
Hethersett	27	TG10
Hetton-le-Hole	45	NZ34
Hetton-le-Hole	41	SE79
Heveningham	27	TM37
Heversham	39	SD48
Hexham	45	NY96
Hexworthy	5	SX67
Heysham	39	SD46
Heytesbury	15	ST94
Heywood	35	SD81
High Bentham	39	SD66
High Ercall	30	SJ51
High Halden	13	TQ83
High Hesket	44	NY44
High Wycome	16	SU89
Higham Ferrers	25	SP96
Highampton	6	SS40
Highbridge	14	ST34
Highcliffe	10	SZ29
Higher Penwortham	34	SD52
Higher Town	4	SV91
Highley	23	SO78
Highworth	15	SU29
Hildenborough	12	TQ54
Hill of Fearn	61	NH87
Hillingdon	17	TQ08
Hillington	26	TF72
Hillswick	63	HU27
Hilton	31	SK23
Himley	23	SO89
Hindhead	11	SU83
Hindley	34	SD60
Hindon	15	ST93
Hingham	27	TG00
Hinkley	24	SP49
Hintlesham	19	TM04
Hirwaun	14	SN90
Hitchin	25	TL12
Hockley Heath	24	SP17
Hockliffe	25	SP92
Hoddesdon	18	TL30
Hodnet	30	SJ62
Holbeach	33	TF32
Holbeton	5	SX65
Holford	14	ST14
Holkham	26	TF84
Holland-on-Sea	19	TM21
Hollingbourne	13	TQ85
Hollingworth	35	SK09
Hollywood	24	SP07
Holmbury St Mary	11	TQ14
Holme Chapel	35	SD82
Holme-upon-Spalding Moor	36	SE83
Holmes Chapel	30	SJ76
Holmfirth	35	SE10
Holmrook	38	SD09
Holne	8	SX76
Holsworthy	6	SS30
Holt	30	SJ45
Holt	27	TG03
Holy Island	49	NU14
Holyhead	28	SH28
Holyhead	28	SH28
Holywell Green	35	SE01
Holywell	29	SJ17
Homersfield	27	TM28
Honeybourne	24	SP14
Honiton	8	ST10
Honley	35	SE11
Hoo	12	TQ77
Hook	15	SU08
Hook	16	SU75
Hope	8	SX63
Hope	31	SK18
Hope under Dinmore	23	SO55
Hopeman	61	NJ16
Hopton-on-Sea	27	TM59
Horley	12	TQ24
Horn's Cross	6	SS32
Hornby	39	SD56
Horncastle	33	TF26
Hornchurch	18	TQ58
Horndean	11	SU71
Horning	27	TG31
Hornsea	37	TA14
Horrabridge	5	SX57
Horringer	19	TL86
Horsehouse	40	SE07
Horsey	27	TG42
Horsforth	35	SE23
Horsham	11	TQ13
Horsington	15	ST62
Horsley Woodhouse	31	SK34
Horton	8	ST31
Horton-cum-Studley	16	SP51
Horton-in-Ribblesdale	39	SD87
Horwich	34	SD61
Hothfield	13	TQ94
Houbie	63	HU69
Hough Green	30	SJ48
Houghton le Spring	45	NZ35
Houghton-on-the-Hill	25	SK60
Hounslow	17	TQ17
Houton	67	HY30
Hove	12	TQ20
Hovingham	40	SE67
Howcaple	23	SO63
Howden	36	SE72
Howden-le-Wear	45	NZ13
Howton	39	NY41
Hoylake	34	SJ28
Hoyland Nether	36	SE30
Hucknall	32	SK54
Huddersfield	35	SE11
Hugh Town	4	SV91
Hull	37	TA02
Hullavington	15	ST88
Humberston	25	SK60
Humbie	48	NT46
Hungerford	16	SU36
Hunmanby	41	TA07
Hunstanton	26	TF64
Hunstrete	15	ST66
Hunters Quay	51	NS17
Huntingdon	25	TL27
Huntley	23	SO71
Huntly	62	NJ53
Hurley	16	SU88
Hurliness	67	ND28
Hurst Green	34	SD63
Hurst Green	12	TQ72
Hurst	16	SU77
Hurstbourne Priors	10	SU44
Hurstbourne Tarrant	16	SU35
Husbands Bosworth	25	SP68
Husborne Crawley	25	SP93
Husinish	64	NA91
Husthwaite	40	SE57
Hutton	34	SD42
Hutton-le-Hole	41	SE79
Huyton	34	SJ49
Hyde	35	SJ99
Hynish	50	NL93
Hythe	10	SU40
Hythe	13	TR13
Ibstock	31	SK41
Ideford	8	SX87
Ilchester	14	ST52
Ilford	18	TQ48
Ilfracombe	6	SS54
Ilkeston	31	SK44
Ilkley	35	SE14
Illingworth	35	SE02
Ilminster	9	ST31
Ilsington	8	SX77
Immingham Dock	37	TA11
Immingham	37	TA11
Inchnadamph	65	NC22
Ingatestone	18	TL60
Ingleton	39	SD67
Ingoldisthorpe	26	TF63
Ingoldmells	33	TF56
Injebrek	38	SC38
Inkberrow	24	SP05
Innellan	51	NS17
Innerleithen	48	NT33
Insch	62	NJ62
Insh	56	NH80
Instow	6	SS43
Inverallochy	63	NK06
Inveraray	51	NN00
Inverey	56	NO08
Inverfarigaig	60	NH52
Invergarry	55	NH30
Invergordon	60	NH66

Inverkeilor	53	NO64
Inverkeithing	48	NT18
Inverkip	51	NS27
Inverkirkaig	65	NC01
Invermoriston	60	NH41
Inverness	60	NH64
Invershin	66	NH59
Inversnaid	51	NN30
Inverurie	57	NJ72
Ipswich	19	TM14
Irby	29	SJ28
Irlam	34	SJ79
Ironbridge	23	SJ60
Irthlingborough	25	SP97
Irvine	47	NS33
Isle of Whithorn	42	NX43
Isle Ornsay	59	NG71
Isleworth	17	TQ17
Iver Heath	17	TQ08
Iver	17	TQ08
Ivinghoe	17	SP91
Ivybridge	5	SX65
Iwade	13	TQ96
Ixworth	27	TL97
Jackton	47	NS55
Jedburgh	49	NT62
Jerbourg	48	GN00
John O'Groats	67	ND37
Johnshaven	57	NO76
Johnstone Bridge	43	NY09
Johnstone	51	NS46
Joohnston	20	SM91
Jurby West	38	SC39
Kames	51	NR97
Kegworth	32	SK42
Keighley	35	SE04
Keiss	67	ND36
Keith	62	NJ45
Keld	39	NY80
Kelso	49	NT73
Kelvedon	19	TL81
Kemble	15	ST99
Kemnay	57	NJ71
Kempston Hardwick	25	TL04
Kempston	25	TL04
Kendal	39	SD59
Kenilworth	24	SP27
Kenmore	52	NN74
Kennacraig	51	NR86
Kennet	52	NS99
Kennethmont	62	NJ52
Kennford	8	SX98
Kenninghall	27	TM08
Kensaleyre	58	NG45
Kentallen	55	NN05
Kentisbeare	7	ST00
Kentra	54	NM66
Kerne Bridge	23	SO51
Kessingland	27	TM58
Keswick	38	NY22
Kettering	25	SP87
Kettlethorpe	35	SE31
Kettletoft	67	HY63
Kettlewell	39	SD97
Keynsham	15	ST66
Kibworth Harcourt	25	SP69
Kidderminster	23	SO87
Kidlington	16	SP41
Kidsgrove	30	SJ85
Kidwelly	21	SN40
Kielder	44	NY69
Kilberry	50	NR76
Kilbirnie	47	NS35
Kilburn	40	SE57
Kilchattan	46	NS05
Kilchiaran	50	NR26
Kilchrenan	51	NN02
Kilcreggan	51	NS28
Kildrummy	57	NJ41
Kildwick	35	SE04
Kilfinan	51	NR97
Kilkhampton	6	SS21
Killearn	52	NS58
Killiecrankie	56	NN96
Killin	52	NN53
Kilmacolm	51	NS36
Kilmaluaig	58	NG47
Kilmarnock	47	NS43
Kilmartin	51	NR89
Kilmaurs	47	NS44
Kilmelford	51	NM81
Kilmore	58	NG60
Kilmory	50	NR77
Kilnhurst	36	SK49
Kilninver	51	NM82
Kilnsea	37	TA41
Kilnsey	39	SD96
Kilsby	24	SP57
Kilsyth	52	NS77
Kilve	7	ST14
Kilwinning	47	NS34
Kimberley	27	TG00
Kimbolton	25	TL16
Kinbrace	66	NC83
Kinbuck	52	NN70
Kincardine	52	NS98
Kincardine O'Neil	57	NO59
Kinclaven	53	NO13
Kincraig	56	NH80
Kineton	24	SP35
King's Bromley	31	SK11
King's Langley	17	TL00
King's Lynn	26	TF62
King's Mills	26	GN00
Kingham	16	SP22
Kinghorn	48	NT28
Kingsbarns	53	NO51
Kingsbridge	8	SX74
Kingsbury	24	SP29
Kingsclere	16	SU55
Kingsdown	13	TR34
Kingseat	52	NT19
Kingsfold	11	TQ13
Kingsgate	13	TR37
Kingskerswell	8	SX86
Kingsley	30	SJ57
Kingstanding	24	SP09
Kingsteignton	8	SX87
Kingston Bagpuize	16	SU49
Kingston	61	NJ36
Kingston upon Thames	17	TQ16
Kingswear	8	SX85
Kingswinford	23	SO88
Kington Langley	15	ST97
Kington	23	SO25
Kingussie	56	NH70
Kinloch Hourn	59	NG90
Kinloch Rannoch	52	NN65
Kinlochard	52	NN40
Kinlochbervie	65	NC25
Kinlocheil	55	NM97
Kinlochewe	59	NH06
Kinlochleven	55	NN16
Kinlochmoidart	54	NM77
Kinloss	61	NJ06
Kinnesswood	53	NO10
Kinross	53	NO10
Kintore	57	NJ71
Kippen	52	NS69
Kirby Fleetham	40	SE29
Kirby Lonsdale	39	SD67
Kirby Misperton	41	SE77
Kirby Stephen	39	NY70
Kirby-in-Furness	38	SD28
Kirkbymoorside	41	SE68
Kirk Langley	31	SK23
Kirk Michael	38	SC39
Kirkbean	43	NX95
Kirkbride	44	NY25
Kirkburton	35	SE11
Kirkby Malzeard	40	SE27
Kirkby	34	SJ49
Kirkby-in-Ashfield	32	SK55
Kirkcaldy	53	NT29
Kirkcolm	42	NX06
Kirkcowan	42	NX36
Kirkcudbright	43	NX65
Kirkham	34	SD43
Kirkhill	60	NH54
Kirkintilloch	47	NS67
Kirkmichael	56	NO06
Kirkmichael	47	NS30
Kirknewton	48	NT16
Kirknewton	49	NT93
Kirkpatrick Fleming	44	NY27
Kirktown of Auchterless	62	NJ74
Kirkwall	67	HY41
Kirkwhelpington	45	NY98
Kirriemuir	53	NO35
Kirton-in-Lindsey	36	SK99
Knaresborough	40	SE35
Knebworth	17	TL22
Knighton	23	SO27
Knightwick	23	SO75
Knipoch	51	NM82
Knockan	65	NC21
Knockandhu	61	NJ22
Knockin	29	SJ32
Knocksharry	38	SC28
Knottingley	36	SE52
Knowle	24	SP17
Knowsley	34	SJ49
Knutsford	30	SJ77
Kyle of Lochalsh	59	NG72
Kyleakin	59	NG72
Kylerhea	59	NG72
Kylestrome	65	NC23
L'Eree	65	GN00
L'Etacq	9	JS00
L'Islet	9	GN00
Laceby	37	TA20
Lady Green	34	SD30
Ladybank	53	NO30
Lagg	50	NR57
Lagg	46	NR92
Laggan Bridge	56	NN69
Laide	64	NG99
Laindon	18	TQ68
Lairg	66	NC50
Lamberhurst	12	TQ63
Lambourn	16	SU37
Lamlash	46	NS03
Lamorna Cove	4	SW42
Lampeter	21	SN54
Lamphey	20	SN00
Lamport	25	SP77
Lanark	47	NS84
Lancaster	39	SD46
Lanchester	45	NZ14
Lancing	11	TQ10
Land's End	4	SW32
Landcross	6	SS42
Langbank	51	NS37
Langho	34	SD73
Langholm	44	NY38
Langland Bay	21	SS68
Langley	17	SU07
Langley Mill	31	SK44
Langley Park	45	NZ24
Langport	14	ST42
Langsett	35	SE20
Langstone	14	ST38
Langthwaite	40	NZ00
Langtoft	33	TF11
Langwathby	44	NY53
Lanivet	5	SX06
Lanreath	5	SX15
Lapford	7	SS70
Lapworth	24	SP17
Largo Ward	53	NO40
Largs	46	NS25
Larkfield	12	TQ75
Larkhall	47	NS75
Lasswade	48	NT36
Lastingham	41	SE79
Latchingdon	19	TL80
Latheron	67	ND23
Lauder	48	NT54
Laugharne	20	SN31
Launceston	5	SX38
Laurencekirk	57	NO77
Laurieston	43	NX66
Lavenham	19	TL94
Laverstoke	10	SU44
Lawers	52	NN63
Lawshall	19	TL85
Laxey	38	SC48
Laxford Bridge	65	NC24
Laxo	63	HU46
Lazonby	44	NY53
Le Bourg	9	GN00
Le Bourg	9	JS00
Leadburn	48	NT25
Leaden Roding	18	TL51
Leadenham	32	SK95
Leadhills	47	NS81
Leamington Spa	24	SP36
Leatherhead	17	TQ15
Lechlade	15	SU29
Leckmelm	65	NH19
Ledbury	23	SO73
Ledmore Junction	65	NC21
Lee Mill	5	SX65
Lee	6	SS44
Lee-on-Solent	10	SU50
Leeds	35	SE33
Leedstown	4	SW63
Leek	31	SJ95
Leekbrook	31	SJ95
Leeming Bar	40	SE28
Leicester	25	SK50
Leigh	34	SD60
Leigh	9	ST60
Leigh	12	TQ54
Leigh-on-Sea	19	TQ88

Leighton Buzzard.................. 16 SP92
Leintwardine...................... 23 SO47
Leiston............................ 19 TM46
Leith.............................. 48 NT27
Lelant............................. 4 SW53
Lendalfoot........................ 42 NX19
Lenham........................... 13 TQ85
Lennoxtown...................... 52 NS67
Lenwade.......................... 27 TG01
Lenzie............................ 47 NS67
Leominster....................... 23 SO45
Lerwick........................... 63 HU44
Les Buttes........................ 9 GN00
Leslie............................. 53 NO20
Leswalt........................... 42 NX06
Letchworth....................... 18 TL23
Letham........................... 53 NO31
Letham........................... 53 NO54
Letterfinlay...................... 55 NN29
Letterston........................ 20 SM92
Leuchars......................... 53 NO42
Leven............................. 53 NO30
Leven............................. 37 TA14
Levens............................ 39 SD48
Lewdown.......................... 5 SX48
Lewes............................. 12 TQ41
Leyburn........................... 40 SE19
Leyland........................... 34 SD52
Leysdown-on-Sea................ 13 TR07
Lichfield.......................... 31 SK10
Lifton.............................. 5 SX38
Lightwater........................ 17 SU96
Lilliesleaf........................ 48 NT52
Limpley Stoke.................... 15 ST76
Lincoln............................ 32 SK97
Lindford........................... 11 SU83
Lingfield.......................... 12 TQ34
Linlithgow........................ 48 NT07
Linslade.......................... 16 SP92
Linton............................. 18 TL54
Linwood........................... 51 NS46
Liphook........................... 11 SU83
Liskeard........................... 5 SX26
Liss............................... 11 SU72
Litherland........................ 34 SJ39
Little Berkhampstead........... 17 TL20
Little Brickhill................... 25 SP93
Little Chalfont.................... 16 SU99
Little Hulton...................... 34 SD70
Little Langdale................... 38 NY30
Little Walsingham................ 27 TF93
Little Weighton................... 37 SE93
Littleborough..................... 35 SD91
Littlebourne...................... 13 TR25
Littlehampton.................... 11 TQ00
Littleport......................... 26 TL58
Littlestone-on-Sea.............. 13 TR02
Liverpool.......................... 34 SJ39
Liversedge........................ 35 SE22
Livingston......................... 48 NT06
Lizard............................. 4 SW71
Llanaelhaearn.................... 28 SH34
Llanaelhaearn.................... 28 SH44
Llanarmon Dyffryn Ceiriog...... 29 SJ13
Llanarth........................... 21 SN45
Llanbedr.......................... 28 SH52
Llanbedr.......................... 29 SJ15
Llanberis.......................... 28 SH56
Llanbister......................... 22 SO17
Llanbrynmair...................... 22 SH80
Llanbydder........................ 21 SN54
Llanddarog....................... 21 SN51
Llandderfel....................... 29 SH93
Llandegai......................... 28 SH66
Llandegla......................... 29 SJ15
Llandeilo.......................... 21 SN62
Llandissilio....................... 20 SN12
Llandogo.......................... 14 SO50
Llandovery........................ 21 SN73
Llandrillo......................... 29 SJ03
Llandrindod Wells................ 22 SO06
Llandudno Junction.............. 29 SH77
Llandudno......................... 29 SH78
Llandybie......................... 21 SN61
Llandyssul........................ 21 SN44
Llanelli........................... 21 SN50
Llanerchymedd.................... 28 SH48
Llanfachraeth.................... 28 SH38
Llanfaethlu....................... 28 SH38
Llanfair Caereinion............. 29 SJ10
Llanfair Dyffryn.................. 29 SJ15
Llanfair Talhaiarn............... 29 SH97
Llanfairfechan.................... 28 SH67
Llanfairpwllgwyngyll............ 28 SH57
Llanfihangel-Nant-Melan......... 22 SO15
Llanfrothen....................... 28 SH64
Llanfyllin......................... 29 SJ11

Llanfynydd........................ 29 SJ25
Llangadfan........................ 29 SJ01
Llangadog......................... 21 SN72
Llangammarch Wells............. 22 SN94
Llangefni.......................... 28 SH47
Llangennith....................... 21 SS49
Llangernyw........................ 29 SH86
Llangoed.......................... 28 SH67
Llangollen......................... 29 SJ24
Llangorse.......................... 22 SO12
Llangranog........................ 20 SN35
Llangurig.......................... 22 SN97
Llangynidr........................ 22 SO11
Llangynog......................... 29 SJ02
Llanharan......................... 14 ST08
Llanidloes......................... 22 SN98
Llanilar........................... 22 SN67
Llanllwni.......................... 21 SN43
Llanon............................. 22 SN56
Llanrhaedr........................ 29 SJ06
Llanrhaedr-ym-Mochnant........ 29 SJ12
Llanrhidian....................... 21 SS49
Llanrhystud....................... 22 SN56
Llanrug............................ 28 SH56
Llanrwst........................... 29 SH76
Llansamlet........................ 21 SS69
Llansannan........................ 29 SH96
Llansantffraid.................... 22 SN56
Llansantffraid-ym-Mechain...... 29 SJ22
Llansawel......................... 21 SN63
Llanstephen....................... 21 SN31
Llanteg............................ 20 SN11
Llanthony......................... 23 SO22
Llantrisant........................ 14 ST08
Llantwit Major.................... 7 SS96
Llanuwchllyn...................... 29 SH82
Llanvetherine..................... 23 SO31
Llanvihangel Crucorney......... 23 SO32
Llanwddyn......................... 29 SJ01
Llanwnda.......................... 28 SH45
Llanwrda.......................... 21 SN73
Llanwrtyd Wells.................. 22 SN84
Llanymynech...................... 29 SJ22
Llechryd........................... 20 SN24
Llwyngwril........................ 28 SH50
Llynclys........................... 29 SJ22
Llyswen........................... 22 SO13
Loanhead.......................... 48 NT26
Lochailort......................... 54 NM78
Lochaline......................... 54 NM64
Locharbriggs...................... 43 NX98
Lochawe........................... 55 NN03
Lochboisdale..................... 64 NF72
Lochbuie........................... 54 NM62
Lochcarron........................ 59 NG83
Lochdonhead...................... 54 NM73
Lochearnhead..................... 52 NN52
Lochgair.......................... 51 NR99
Lochgelly.......................... 53 NT19
Lochgilphead..................... 51 NR88
Lochgoilhead..................... 51 NN20
Lochinver......................... 65 NC02
Lochmaben........................ 43 NY08
Lochranza......................... 46 NR95
Lochwinnoch...................... 47 NS35
Lockerbie.......................... 43 NY18
Lockmaddy........................ 58 NF96
Loddon............................ 27 TM39
Loe................................ 5 SX25
Lofthouse......................... 35 SE32
Loftus............................. 41 NZ71
Lolworth........................... 18 TL36
London............................ 17 TQ38
Long Crendon...................... 16 SP60
Long Eaton........................ 32 SK43
Long Hanborough................. 16 SP41
Long Melford...................... 19 TL84
Long Preston...................... 39 SD85
Long Stratton..................... 27 TM19
Long Sutton....................... 33 TF42
Longbridge Deverill.............. 15 ST84
Longdown.......................... 8 SX89
Longformacus..................... 49 NT65
Longframlington.................. 45 NU10
Longham........................... 10 SZ09
Longhorsley....................... 45 NZ19
Longhoughton..................... 49 NU21
Longnor............................ 23 SJ40
Longnor............................ 31 SK06
Longridge......................... 34 SD63
Longton........................... 34 SD42
Longton........................... 30 SJ94
Longville.......................... 23 SO59
Lossiemouth....................... 61 NJ27
Lostwithiel........................ 5 SX15
Loughborough..................... 32 SK51
Loughor........................... 21 SS59

Loughton........................... 18 TQ49
Louth.............................. 33 TF38
Low Eggborough.................. 36 SE52
Lowdham........................... 32 SK64
Lower Barvas...................... 64 NB45
Lower Beeding..................... 11 TQ22
Lower Brailes..................... 24 SP33
Lower Slaughter................... 24 SP12
Lowestoft.......................... 27 TM59
Loweswater........................ 38 NY12
Lowick............................. 49 NU03
Ludborough........................ 37 TF29
Luddenden......................... 35 SE02
Ludgershall....................... 10 SU25
Ludlow............................. 23 SO57
Ludwell........................... 15 ST92
Ludworth.......................... 45 NZ34
Lugton............................. 47 NS45
Lugwardine........................ 23 SO54
Lumbly............................ 36 SE43
Lumphanan......................... 57 NJ50
Lumsden........................... 57 NJ42
Lunan Bay......................... 53 NO65
Lundin Links...................... 53 NO40
Luss.............................. 51 NS39
Lustleigh.......................... 8 SX78
Luton Airport...................... 17 TL12
Luton.............................. 17 TL02
Lutterworth....................... 24 SP58
Lybster............................ 67 ND23
Lydd.............................. 13 TR02
Lyddington........................ 25 SP89
Lydford............................ 5 SX58
Lydford-on-Fosse................. 14 ST53
Lydham........................... 23 SO39
Lydiate........................... 34 SD30
Lydney............................ 15 SO60
Lye................................ 24 SO98
Lyme Regis........................ 9 SY39
Lyminge........................... 13 TR14
Lymington......................... 10 SZ39
Lymm.............................. 30 SJ68
Lympsham......................... 14 ST35
Lyndhurst......................... 10 SU20
Lyneham........................... 15 SU07
Lyness............................ 67 ND39
Lynmouth.......................... 6 SS74
Lynton............................. 6 SS74
Lytham St Annes.................. 34 SD32

Mablethorpe....................... 33 TF58
Macclesfield...................... 30 SJ97
Macduff........................... 62 NJ76
Machrie........................... 46 NR83
Machrihanish...................... 46 NR62
Machynlleth....................... 22 SH70
Maerdy............................ 14 SS99
Maesteg........................... 21 SS89
Magor............................. 14 ST48
Maiden Bradley.................... 15 ST83
Maiden Newton..................... 9 SY59
Maidencombe...................... 8 SX96
Maidenhead....................... 16 SU88
Maidstone......................... 12 TQ75
Maidwell.......................... 25 SP77
Mainsriddle....................... 43 NX95
Maldon............................ 19 TL80
Malham............................ 39 SD86
Mallaig........................... 54 NM69
Mallwyd........................... 29 SH81
Malmesbury....................... 15 ST98
Malpas............................ 30 SJ44
Maltby............................ 36 SK59
Malton............................ 41 SE77
Malvern........................... 23 SO74
Manaccan.......................... 4 SW72
Manchester Airport............... 30 SJ88
Manchester........................ 35 SJ89
Manea............................. 26 TL48
Manorbier......................... 20 SS09
Mansfield......................... 32 SK56
Mansfield Woodhouse............. 32 SK56
Manston........................... 13 TR36
Manuden.......................... 18 TL42
Mapperley......................... 31 SK44
Marazion.......................... 4 SW53
March............................. 26 TL49
Marcham........................... 16 SU49
Marchwiel......................... 30 SJ34
Marchwood......................... 10 SU31
Marden............................ 12 TQ74
Mareham-le-Fen................... 33 TF26
Maresfield......................... 12 TQ42
Marford........................... 30 SJ35
Margate........................... 13 TR37
Marianglas........................ 28 SH58

Market Bosworth	24 SK40	Milford-on-Sea	10 SZ29	Nailsea	14 ST47
Market Deeping	33 TF11	Millbrook	9 JS00	Nailsworth	15 ST89
Market Drayton	30 SJ63	Millbrook	5 SX45	Nairn	61 NH85
Market Harborough	25 SP78	Millhouse	51 NR77	Nant-Ddu	22 SO01
Market Rasen	37 TF18	Millom	38 SD18	Nantgarw	14 ST18
Market Weighton	36 SE84	Milnathort	53 NO10	Nantwich	30 SJ65
Markfield	32 SK41	Milngavie	47 NS57	Narberth	20 SN11
Markham Moor	32 SK77	Milnrow	35 SD91	Narborough	24 SP59
Markham	14 SO10	Milnthorpe	39 SD48	Narborough	26 TF71
Markinch	53 NO30	Milovaig	58 NG15	Nayland	19 TL93
Markington	40 SE26	Milton Abbas	9 ST80	Neasham	40 NZ31
Marks Tey	19 TL92	Milton Common	16 SP60	Neath	21 SS79
Markyate	17 TL01	Milton Ernest	25 TL05	Needham Market	19 TM05
Marlborough	15 SU16	Milton Keynes	25 SP83	Nefyn	28 SH34
Marldon	8 SX86	Milton	20 SN00	Nelson	35 SD83
Marley Hill	45 NZ25	Milton-on-Stour	15 ST82	Nesscliffe	30 SJ31
Marlow	16 SU88	Minchinhampton	15 SO80	Neston	29 SJ27
Marnhull	9 ST71	Minehead	7 SS94	Nether Broughton	32 SK72
Marple	35 SJ98	Minera	29 SJ25	Nethy Bridge	56 NJ02
Marsden	35 SE01	Minster Lovell	16 SP31	Nettlebed	16 SU68
Marshfield	15 ST77	Minster	13 TR36	Nevern	20 SN03
Marske-by-the-Sea	40 NZ62	Minsterley	23 SJ30	New Abbey	43 NX96
Marston Magna	15 ST52	Mintlaw	63 NK04	New Aberdour	62 NJ86
Marston Moretaine	25 SP94	Mirfield	35 SE21	New Blyth	62 NJ85
Marston Trussell	25 SP68	Miskin	14 ST08	New Brighton	34 SJ39
Martham	27 TG41	Misterton	36 SK79	New Buckenham	27 TM09
Martinhoe	6 SS64	Mitcham	17 TQ26	New Cumnock	47 NS61
Martock	9 ST41	Mitcheldean	23 SO61	New Deer	62 NJ84
Marton	40 NZ51	Mobberley	30 SJ77	New Galloway	43 NX67
Mary Tavy	5 SX57	Mochdre	29 SH87	New Grimsby	4 SV81
Marykirk	57 NO66	Mochrum	42 NX34	New Holland	37 TA02
Maryport	43 NY03	Modbury	5 SX65	New Luce	42 NX16
Masham	40 SE28	Moffat	43 NT00	New Malden	17 TQ26
Matlock Bath	31 SK25	Mold	29 SJ26	New Mills	31 SK08
Matlock	31 SK26	Moniaive	43 NX79	New Milton	10 SZ29
Mattingley	16 SU75	Monifieth	53 NO43	New Pitsligo	62 NJ85
Mauchline	47 NS52	Monk Fryston	36 SE52	New Quay	21 SN35
Maughold	38 SC49	Monkleigh	6 SS42	New Radnor	22 SO26
Mawgan Porth	4 SW86	Monks Eleigh	19 TL94	New Romney	13 TR02
Mawnan Smith	4 SW72	Monmouth	23 SO51	New Scone	52 NO12
Maybole	47 NS30	Montacute	9 ST41	Newark-on-Trent	32 SK75
Mayfield	12 TQ52	Montgomery	23 SO29	Newbiggin	39 NY92
Maypool	8 SX85	Montrose	53 NO75	Newbiggin-by-the-Sea	45 NZ38
Mealsgate	43 NY24	Monymusk	57 NJ61	Newbigging	53 NO43
Measham	31 SK31	Moorlinch	14 ST33	Newbold-upon-Stour	24 SP24
Medbourne	25 SP79	Morar	54 NM69	Newborough	28 SH46
Meigle	53 NO24	Morden	17 TQ26	Newbridge	48 NT17
Melbourn	18 TL34	Mordiford	23 SO53	Newbridge	16 SP40
Melksham	15 ST96	Morebattle	49 NT72	Newbridge-on-Wye	22 SO05
Melling	39 SD57	Morecambe	39 SD46	Newburgh	63 NJ92
Melmerby	44 NY63	Morecombelake	9 SY49	Newburgh	53 NO21
Melmerby	40 SE37	Moreton-in-Marsh	24 SP23	Newburn	45 NZ16
Melrose	48 NT53	Moretonhampstead	5 SX78	Newbury	16 SU46
Meltham	35 SE01	Morfa Nefyn	28 SH24	Newby Bridge	39 SD38
Melton	36 SE92	Morley	35 SE22	Newcastle Emlyn	20 SN34
Melton Constable	27 TG03	Morningside	48 NT27	Newcastle upon Tyne Airport.	45 NZ17
Melton Mowbray	32 SK71	Morpeth	45 NZ18	Newcastle upon Tyne	45 NZ26
Melvaig	59 NG78	Morriston	21 SS69	Newcastle-under-Lyme	30 SJ84
Melvich	66 NC86	Mortehoe	6 SS44	Newcastleton	44 NY48
Membury	8 ST20	Morville	23 SO69	Newenden	13 TQ82
Membury	16 SU37	Morwenstow	6 SS21	Newent	23 SO72
Memsie	63 NJ96	Mossat	57 NJ41	Newgale	20 SM82
Menai Bridge	28 SH57	Mossley	35 SD90	Newgate Street	17 TL30
Mere	30 SJ78	Mostyn	29 SJ18	Newhaven	31 SK16
Mere	15 ST83	Motherwell	47 NS75	Newhaven	12 TQ40
Meriden	24 SP28	Mottram St Andrew	30 SJ87	Newhouse	47 NS76
Merstham	11 TQ25	Mottram-in-Longdendale	35 SJ99	Newington	13 TQ86
Merthyr Tydfil	14 SO00	Moulsford	16 SU58	Newlyn	4 SW42
Messingham	36 SE80	Mount Hawke	4 SW74	Newmains	47 NS85
Metheringham	33 TF06	Mountain Ash	14 ST09	Newmarket	18 TL66
Methlick	62 NJ83	Mountsorrel	32 SK51	Newmill on Teviot	44 NT41
Methven	52 NO02	Mousehole	4 SW42	Newnham	23 SO66
Methwold	26 TL79	Moy	60 NH73	Newport Pagnell	25 SP84
Mevagissey	4 SX04	Much Birch	23 SO53	Newport	30 SJ71
Mexborough	36 SE40	Much Hadham	18 TL41	Newport	20 SN03
Micheldever	10 SU53	Much Hoole	34 SD42	Newport	14 ST38
Mickleton	24 SP14	Much Wenlock	23 SO69	Newport	10 SZ48
Mid Yell	63 HU59	Muchalls	57 NO99	Newport	18 TL53
Middle Town	4 SV80	Mudeford	10 SZ19	Newport-on-Tay	53 NO42
Middle Wallop	10 SU23	Muir of Ord	60 NH55	Newquay	4 SW86
Middleham	40 SE18	Muirdrum	53 NO53	Newton Abbot	8 SX87
Middlesbrough	40 NZ42	Muirhead	47 NS67	Newton Aycliffe	40 NZ22
Middleton	50 NL94	Muirhead	53 NO33	Newton Ferrers	5 SX54
Middleton	35 SD80	Muirkirk	47 NS62	Newton Linford	32 SK51
Middleton Stoney	16 SP52	Mullion Cove	4 SW61	Newton Poppleford	8 SY08
Middleton-in-Teesdale	39 NY92	Mullion	4 SW61	Newton Solney	31 SK22
Middleton-on-Sea	11 SU90	Mumbles	21 SS68	Newton St Cyres	8 SX89
Middleton-on-the Wolds	36 SE94	Mundesley-on-Sea	27 TG33	Newton Stewart	42 NX46
Middlewich	30 SJ76	Mundford	26 TL89	Newton-le-Willows	34 SJ59
Midhurst	11 SU82	Mundon Hill	19 TL80	Newton-on-Trent	32 SK87
Midsomer Norton	15 ST65	Mungrisdale	44 NY33	Newtonmore	56 NN79
Midtown Brae	59 NG88	Munslow	23 SO58	Newtown	22 SO19
Milborne St Andrew	9 SY89	Murton	45 NZ34	Newtown	23 SO64
Mildenhall	26 TL77	Musselburgh	48 NT37	Newtown	10 SU61
Milesmark	52 NT08	Muthill	52 NN81	Newtown Linford	32 SK51
Milford Haven	20 SM90	Mybster	67 ND25	Newtyle	53 NO24
Milford	11 SU94	Mytholmroyd	35 SE02	Neyland	20 SM90

Nigg	61	NH87
Ninfield	12	TQ71
Niton	10	SZ57
Nolton Haven	20	SM81
Norden	35	SD81
Norham	49	NT94
Norman Cross	25	TL19
Normanton	36	SE32
Normanton	32	SK90
North Ballachulish	55	NN06
North Berwick	48	NT58
North Bragar	64	NB24
North Coates	37	TA30
North Elmham	27	TF92
North Erradale	59	NG78
North Ferriby	37	SE92
North Grimston	41	SE86
North Huish	8	SX75
North Kyme	33	TF15
North Molton	7	SS72
North Muskham	32	SK75
North Petherton	14	ST23
North Queensferry	48	NT18
North Roe	63	HU38
North Shields	42	NZ36
North Somercotes	37	TF49
North Stifford	12	TQ68
North Stoke	16	SU68
North Tawton	6	SS60
North Tolsta	64	NB54
North Tuddenham	27	TG01
North Walsham	27	TG23
North Waltham	10	SU54
North Warnborough	11	SU75
Northallerton	40	SE39
Northam	6	SS42
Northampton	25	SP76
Northfleet	12	TQ67
Northiam	13	TQ82
Northleach	24	SP11
Northop	29	SJ26
Northop Hall	29	SJ26
Northwich	30	SJ67
Northwood	17	TQ09
Norton	41	SE77
Norton	23	SJ70
Norton St Philip	15	ST75
Norwich	27	TG20
Norwick	63	HP61
Nottingham	32	SK53
Nuneaton	24	SP39
Nunney Catch	15	ST74
Nutfield	12	TQ35
Oadby	25	SK60
Oakengates	30	SJ71
Oakham	32	SK80
Oakley	16	SP61
Oakley	10	SU55
Oakley	25	TL05
Oakworth	35	SE03
Oban	54	NM83
Ochiltree	47	NS52
Odiham	11	SU75
Ogbourne St. George	15	SU27
Ogmore-by-Sea	21	SS87
Okehampton	6	SX59
Old Deer	63	NJ94
Old Grimsby	4	SV81
Old Leake	33	TF45
Old Meldrum	62	NJ82
Old Rayne	62	NJ62
Old Sodbury	15	ST78
Old Town	4	SV91
Old Windsor	17	SU97
Oldbury	24	SO98
Oldcotes	36	SK58
Oldham	35	SD90
Ollaberry	63	HU38
Olney	25	SP85
Ombersley	23	SO86
Onchan	38	SC47
Ongar	18	TL50
Onich	55	NN06
Ord	58	NG61
Orford	19	TM45
Orgil	67	HY20
Ormesby	27	TG41
Ormskirk	34	SD40
Orpington	12	TQ46
Orsett	12	TQ68
Osmington	9	SY78
Osmotherley	40	SE49
Ossett	35	SE22
Osterley	17	TQ17
Oswaldkirk	40	SE67

Oswaldtwistle	35	SD72
Oswestry	29	SJ22
Otford	12	TQ55
Othery	14	ST33
Otley	35	SE24
Otterburn	45	NY89
Ottery St Mary	8	SY19
Oulton Broad	27	TM59
Oulton Park	30	SJ56
Oulton	36	SE32
Oundle	25	TL08
Outlane	35	SE01
Outwell	26	TF50
Over	30	SJ66
Overseal	31	SK21
Overstrand	27	TG24
Overton	10	SU54
Overton-on-Dee	30	SJ34
Ovington	45	NZ06
Oxenhope	35	SE03
Oxford	16	SP50
Oxted	12	TQ35
Oxton	32	SK65
Paddock Wood	12	TQ64
Padiham	35	SD73
Padstow	4	SW97
Pagham	11	SZ89
Paignton	8	SX86
Painswick	15	SO80
Paisley	47	NS46
Pangbourne	16	SU67
Pannal	35	SE25
Pant-y-Dwr	22	SN97
Par	5	SX05
Parbold	34	SD41
Parkeston Quay	19	TM23
Parkgate	29	SJ27
Parkham	6	SS32
Parkhurst	10	SZ49
Parson Drove	33	TF30
Partick	47	NS56
Partington	34	SJ79
Partridge Green	11	TQ11
Pateley Bridge	40	SE16
Patrick	38	SC28
Patrington	37	TA32
Patterdale	39	NY31
Pattingham	23	SO89
Paulton	15	ST65
Peacehaven	12	TQ40
Peasedown St John	15	ST75
Peasmarsh	13	TQ82
Peebles	48	NT24
Peel	38	SC28
Pelynt	5	SX25
Pembridge	23	SO35
Pembroke Dock	20	SM90
Pembroke	20	SM90
Pen-y-gwryd	28	SH65
Penarth	14	ST17
Pencaitland	48	NT46
Pencoed	21	SS98
Pencraig	23	SO52
Pendeen	4	SW33
Pendine	20	SN20
Pendlebury	35	SD70
Pendoggett	4	SX07
Penicuik	48	NT26
Penistone	35	SE20
Penketh	34	SJ58
Penkridge	30	SJ91
Penllergaer	21	SS69
Penmachno	29	SH75
Penmaen	21	SS58
Penmaenmawr	28	SH77
Pennal	22	SH70
Pennard	21	SS58
Penthiwllan	21	SN34
Penrhyndeudraeth	28	SH63
Penrith	44	NY53
Penryn	4	SW73
Pensarn	21	SN41
Penshurst	12	TQ54
Pentewan	4	SX04
Pentre Halkyn	29	SJ27
Pentrefoelas	29	SH85
Penybont	22	SO16
Penybontfawr	29	SJ02
Penygroes	28	SH45
Penzance	4	SW43
Perelle	4	GN00
Perivale	17	TQ18
Perranporth	4	SW75
Perranuthnoe	4	SW52
Perry Bar	24	SP09

Pershore	24	SO94
Perth	52	NO12
Peterborough	25	TL19
Peterchurch	23	SO33
Peterculter	57	NJ80
Peterhead	63	NK14
Petersfield	11	SU72
Peterstow	23	SO52
Petts Wood	12	TQ46
Petty France	15	ST78
Petworth	11	SU92
Pevensey	12	TQ60
Pewsey	15	SU15
Pickering	41	SE78
Picket Post	10	SU10
Piddletrenthide	9	SY79
Piercebridge	40	NZ21
Pierowall	67	HY44
Pill	14	ST57
Pillerton Priors	24	SP24
Pilning	14	ST58
Pimperne	9	ST90
Pinchbeck	33	TF22
Pinner	17	TQ18
Pinwherry	42	NX18
Pirnmill	46	NR84
Pitcaple	62	NJ72
Pitlochry	52	NN95
Pitmedden	62	NJ82
Pitsea	18	TQ78
Pittenweem	53	NO50
Pleasley	32	SK56
Pleinmont	32	GN00
Plemont	9	JS00
Plockton	59	NG83
Plymouth	5	SX45
Plympton	5	SX55
Pocklington	36	SE84
Podimore	14	ST52
Polbain	64	NB91
Polegate	12	TQ50
Polmont	52	NS97
Polperro	5	SX25
Polruan	5	SX15
Polzeath	4	SW97
Ponders End	17	TQ39
Pontardawe	21	SN70
Pontardulais	21	SN50
Pontefract	36	SE42
Ponteland	45	NZ17
Pontesbury	30	SJ30
Pontfadog	29	SJ23
Pontllanfraith	14	ST19
Pontnewydd	14	ST29
Pontrhydfendigaid	22	SN76
Pontrilas	23	SO32
Pontyates	21	SN40
Pontyberem	21	SN51
Pontypool	14	SO20
Pontypridd	14	ST09
Pool-in-Wharfedale	35	SE24
Poole	10	SZ09
Poolewe	59	NG88
Pooley Bridge	39	NY42
Porlock	7	SS84
Porlock Weir	7	SS84
Port Appin	54	NM94
Port Askaig	50	NR46
Port Charlotte	50	NR25
Port Ellen	50	NR34
Port Erin	38	SC16
Port Eynon	21	SS48
Portgaverne	4	SX08
Port Glasgow	51	NS37
Port Henderson	59	NG77
Port Isaac	4	SW98
Port Logan	42	NX04
Port of Menteith	52	NN50
Port William	42	NX34
Port of Ness	64	NB56
Port Soderick	38	SC37
Port St Mary	38	SC26
Port Talbot	21	SS78
Portchester	10	SU60
Portdinorwic	28	SH56
Portelet Bay	9	JS00
Porthcawl	21	SS87
Porthcurno	4	SW32
Porthkerry	7	ST06
Porthleven	4	SW62
Porthmadog	28	SH53
Porthtowan	4	SW64
Porthyrhyd	21	SN51
Portishead	14	ST47
Portknockie	62	NJ46
Portland	9	SY67
Portlethen	57	NO99

Portloe................................ 4 SW93
Portmahomack................. 61 NH98
Portnacroish.................... 55 NM94
Portnahaven..................... 50 NR15
Portpatrick...................... 42 NX05
Portreath......................... 4 SW64
Portree............................ 58 NG44
Portscatho....................... 4 SW83
Portslade-by-Sea............. 12 TQ20
Portsmouth...................... 11 SZ69
Portsoy........................... 62 NJ56
Portwrinkle...................... 5 SX35
Postcombe....................... 16 SU79
Pott Shrigley................... 31 SJ97
Potter Heigham............... 27 TG41
Potters Bar...................... 17 TL20
Potton............................. 18 TL24
Poulton-le-Flyde.............. 23 SO33
Poundsgate...................... 8 SX77
Powburn.......................... 49 NU01
Powfoot.......................... 43 NY16
Powick............................ 23 SO85
Powmill........................... 52 NT09
Powmill........................... 52 NT09
Poynton.......................... 30 SJ98
Praa Sands...................... 4 SW52
Praze-an-Beeble............... 4 SW63
Prees Health.................... 30 SJ53
Preesall........................... 34 SD34
Prenteg........................... 28 SH54
Prescot............................ 34 SJ49
Prestatyn......................... 29 SJ08
Prestbury......................... 30 SJ87
Presteigne....................... 23 SO36
Preston Gubbals............... 30 SJ41
Preston........................... 49 NT75
Preston........................... 34 SD53
Prestwich........................ 35 SD80
Prestwick........................ 47 NS32
Princes Risborough.......... 16 SP80
Princethorpe................... 24 SP47
Princetown...................... 5 SX57
Prudhoe.......................... 45 NZ06
Puckeridge...................... 18 TL32
Puddletown..................... 9 SY79
Pudsey............................ 35 SE23
Pulborough...................... 11 TQ01
Pumsaint......................... 21 SN64
Purfleet........................... 12 TQ57
Purley............................. 12 TQ36
Pwllheli........................... 28 SH33
Pyle................................ 21 SS88

Queen's Park................... 47 NS56
Queenborough.................. 13 TQ97
Queensbury..................... 35 SE13
Queensferry..................... 29 SJ36
Quendon.......................... 18 TL53
Quorn.............................. 32 SK51

Raasay............................ 58 NG53
Radcliffe......................... 35 SD70
Radcliffe-on-Trent............ 32 SK63
Radlett............................ 17 TL10
Radstock......................... 15 ST65
Radwinter........................ 18 TL63
Rafford........................... 61 NJ05
Raglan............................ 14 SO40
Rainford.......................... 34 SD40
Rainham.......................... 12 TQ58
Rainhill........................... 34 SJ49
Rame............................... 4 SW73
Ramsbottom.................... 35 SD71
Ramsey............................ 38 SC49
Ramsey............................ 26 TL28
Ramsey............................ 19 TM23
Ramsgate......................... 13 TR36
Ramsgill.......................... 40 SE17
Rangemore....................... 31 SK12
Rangeworthy.................... 15 ST68
Rannoch Station............... 55 NN45
Ranworth......................... 27 TG31
Rapness.......................... 67 HY54
Rattray........................... 53 NO14
Ravenglass...................... 38 SD09
Ravenstonedale............... 39 NY70
Rawmarsh........................ 36 SK49
Rawreth.......................... 18 TQ79
Rawtenstall...................... 35 SD82
Rayleigh.......................... 18 TQ89
Read............................... 35 SD73
Reading........................... 16 SU77
Rearsby........................... 32 SK61
Reay............................... 66 NC96
Red Row.......................... 45 NZ29

Red Wharf Bay................. 28 SH58
Redbourn......................... 17 TL11
Redbrook......................... 30 SJ54
Redcar............................. 40 NZ62
Redditch.......................... 24 SP06
Redhill............................ 12 TQ25
Redland........................... 67 HY32
Redmile........................... 32 SK73
Redruth........................... 4 SW64
Reedham.......................... 27 TG40
Reepham.......................... 27 TG02
Reeth.............................. 40 SE09
Reiff............................... 64 NB91
Reigate............................ 12 TQ25
Reighton.......................... 41 TA17
Rempstone....................... 32 SK52
Renfrew........................... 47 NS56
Renishaw......................... 31 SK47
Resolven.......................... 21 SN80
Retford............................ 32 SK78
Rettendon........................ 18 TQ79
Reynoldston...................... 21 SS49
Rhayader.......................... 22 SN96
Rhiconich......................... 65 NC25
Rhoose............................ 7 ST06
Rhos............................... 21 SN33
Rhos-on-Sea..................... 29 SH88
Rhosneigr........................ 28 SH37
Rhossili........................... 21 SS48
Rhu................................ 51 NS28
Rhubodach....................... 51 NS07
Rhuddlan......................... 29 SJ07
Rhydowen........................ 21 SN44
Rhyd-ddu......................... 28 SH55
Rhyl............................... 29 SJ08
Rhymney.......................... 14 SO10
Rhynie............................ 62 NJ42
Ribchester....................... 34 SD63
Richard's Castle............... 23 SO46
Richmond......................... 40 NZ10
Richmond upon Thames..... 17 TQ17
Rickmansworth................. 17 TQ09
Ridsdale.......................... 45 NY98
Rillington........................ 41 SE87
Ringford.......................... 43 NX65
Ringsall.......................... 17 SP91
Ringwood......................... 10 SU10
Ripley............................. 40 SE26
Ripley............................. 31 SK45
Ripley............................. 17 TQ05
Ripon.............................. 40 SE37
Ripple............................. 23 SO83
Ripponden....................... 35 SE01
Risca.............................. 14 ST29
Risegate.......................... 33 TF22
Riseley............................ 25 TL06
Rishton............................ 34 SD73
Risley............................. 31 SK43
Roadhead......................... 44 NY57
Roberton......................... 47 NS92
Robertsbridge................... 12 TQ72
Robeston Wathen.............. 20 SN01
Robin Hood's Bay.............. 41 NZ90
Rocester.......................... 31 SK13
Rochdale......................... 35 SD81
Rochester......................... 44 NY89
Rochester-upon-Medway.... 12 TQ76
Rochford.......................... 19 TQ89
Rock............................... 4 SW97
Rockbeare........................ 8 SY09
Rockcliffe......................... 43 NX85
Rockingham...................... 25 SP89
Roewen........................... 28 SH77
Rogart............................. 66 NC70
Rogerstone...................... 14 ST28
Rolvenden........................ 13 TQ83
Romaldkirk....................... 39 NY92
Romford........................... 18 TQ58
Romsey............................ 10 SU32
Romsley........................... 24 SO97
Rookhope......................... 45 NY94
Rooksbridge...................... 14 ST35
Ropley............................. 11 SU63
Rosebank......................... 47 NS84
Rosedale Abbey................ 41 SE79
Rosehall.......................... 65 NC40
Rosehearty....................... 63 NJ96
Rosemarkie....................... 60 NH75
Ross-on-Wye..................... 23 SO52
Rossett............................ 30 SJ35
Rossington....................... 36 SK69
Rosthwaite....................... 38 NY21
Rothbury.......................... 45 NU00
Rotherham........................ 36 SK49
Rotherwick....................... 16 SU75
Rothes............................. 61 NJ24
Rothesay.......................... 51 NS06

Rothley............................ 32 SK51
Rothwell.......................... 35 SE32
Rothwell.......................... 25 SP88
Rottingdean..................... 12 TQ30
Roughton......................... 27 TG23
Rousdon........................... 8 SY29
Row................................ 5 SX07
Rowardennan.................... 51 NS39
Rowen............................. 28 SH77
Rowlands Castle............... 11 SU71
Rowlands Gill................... 45 NZ15
Rowley Regis.................... 24 SO98
Rowsley........................... 31 SK26
Rowstock......................... 16 SU48
Roxburgh......................... 49 NT63
Roy Bridge....................... 55 NN28
Royston........................... 36 SE31
Royston........................... 18 TL34
Royton............................ 35 SD90
Rozel Bay......................... 9 JS00
Ruabon........................... 29 SJ34
Ruan High Lanes............... 4 SW94
Ruan Minor...................... 4 SW71
Rubery............................ 24 SO97
Rudgwick......................... 11 TQ03
Rudston........................... 41 TA06
Rufford............................ 34 SD41
Rugby............................. 24 SP57
Rugeley........................... 31 SK01
Ruislip............................ 17 TQ08
Rumney........................... 14 ST27
Runcorn........................... 30 SJ58
Rushden.......................... 25 SP96
Rushlake Green................. 12 TQ61
Rushyford......................... 40 NZ22
Rusper............................ 11 TQ23
Rustington....................... 11 TQ00
Ruswarp.......................... 41 NZ80
Rutherglen....................... 47 NS66
Ruthin............................. 29 SJ15
Ruthwell.......................... 43 NY06
Ruyton-XI-Towns.............. 30 SJ32
Ryde............................... 10 SZ59
Rye................................ 13 TQ92
Ryhope............................ 45 NZ45
Ryton.............................. 45 NZ16

Sacriston......................... 45 NZ24
Sadberge......................... 40 NZ31
Saddell........................... 46 NR73
Saffron Walden................. 18 TL53
Salcombe Regis................ 8 SY18
Salcombe......................... 8 SX73
Sale................................ 35 SJ79
Salen.............................. 54 NM66
Salford............................ 35 SJ89
Salhouse.......................... 27 TG31
Saline.............................. 52 NT09
Salisbury......................... 10 SU12
Saltash............................ 5 SX45
Saltburn-by-the-Sea.......... 40 NZ62
Saltcoats......................... 46 NS24
Saltfleet.......................... 37 TF49
Saltfleetby....................... 37 TF49
Salthouse........................ 27 TG04
Sampford Peverell............ 7 ST01
Sandbach......................... 30 SJ76
Sandbanks........................ 10 SZ08
Sanderstead..................... 12 TQ35
Sandford.......................... 14 ST45
Sandgarth......................... 67 HY51
Sandhaven........................ 63 NJ96
Sandhead........................ 42 NX04
Sandiacre......................... 32 SK43
Sandiway......................... 30 SJ67
Sandness......................... 63 HU15
Sandown.......................... 10 SZ58
Sandringham..................... 26 TF62
Sandsend......................... 41 NZ81
Sandwich......................... 13 TR35
Sandy.............................. 25 TL14
Sandycroft....................... 29 SJ36
Sandygate........................ 38 SC39
Sanquhar......................... 47 NS70
Sarn............................... 28 SH23
Sarnesfield....................... 23 SO35
Sarre.............................. 13 TR26
Sartfield.......................... 38 SC39
Saughtree........................ 44 NY59
Saul............................... 15 SO70
Saundersfoot.................... 20 SN10
Saunderton...................... 16 SP70
Saunton.......................... 6 SS43
Sawbridgeworth................ 18 TL41
Sawston.......................... 18 TL44
Saxby............................. 32 SK81

Saxmundham 19 TM36
Saxthorpe 27 TG13
Scalasaig 50 NR39
Scalby 41 TA09
Scalloway 63 HU43
Scampton 32 SK97
Scarborough 41 TA08
Scarinish 50 NM04
Scarisbrick 34 SD31
Scarista 58 NG09
Scawby 36 SE90
Scole 27 TM17
Scone 53 NO12
Sconser 58 NG53
Scopwick 33 TF05
Scorton 40 NZ20
Scotch Corner 40 NZ20
Scots' Gap 45 NZ08
Scourie 65 NC14
Scrabster 67 ND17
Scunthorpe 36 SE81
Sea Palling 27 TG41
Seaford 12 TV49
Seaham 45 NZ44
Seahouses 49 NU23
Seale 11 SU84
Seamer 41 TA08
Seamill 46 NS14
Seascale 38 NY00
Seathwaite 38 SD29
Seatoller 38 NY21
Seaton Burn 45 NZ27
Seaton Carew 40 NZ52
Seaton 8 SY29
Seaview 11 SZ69
Sedbergh 39 SD69
Sedgeberrow 24 SP03
Sedgebrook 32 SK83
Sedgefield 40 NZ32
Sedgemoor S A 14 ST35
Sedgley 24 SO99
Sedlescombe 12 TQ71
Selborne 11 SU73
Selby 36 SE63
Selkirk 48 NT42
Selly Oak 24 SP08
Selsey 11 SZ89
Selstead 13 TR24
Senghenydd 14 ST19
Sennen 4 SW32
Sennybridge 22 SN92
Settle 39 SD86
Sevenoaks 12 TQ55
Shaftesbury 15 ST82
Shaldon 8 SX97
Shalfleet 10 SZ48
Shandon 51 NS28
Shanklin 10 SZ58
Shap 39 NY51
Shapwick 14 ST43
Shardlow 31 SK43
Sharnbrook 25 SP95
Sharnford 24 SP49
Sharpness 15 SO60
Shaw 35 SD90
Shawbury 30 SJ52
Shawell 24 SP58
Sheerness 13 TQ97
Sheerwater 17 TQ06
Sheffield 31 SK38
Shefford 25 TL13
Sheldon 24 SP18
Shelf 35 SE12
Shenstone 24 SK10
Shepley 35 SE10
Shepperton 17 TQ06
Shepshed 32 SK41
Shepton Mallet 15 ST64
Sheraton 45 NZ43
Sherborne 9 ST61
Sherburn 41 SE97
Sherburn-in-Elmet 36 SE43
Sheriff Hutton 40 SE66
Sheringham 27 TG14
Sherston 15 ST88
Shevington 34 SD50
Shieldaig 59 NG85
Shifnal 30 SJ70
Shildon 40 NZ22
Shillingford 16 SU59
Shipdham 27 TF90
Shipham 14 ST45
Shiplake 16 SU77
Shipley 35 SE13
Shipston-on-Stour 24 SP24
Shipton-under-Wychwood .. 16 SP21
Shiptonthorpe 36 SE84

Shiremoor 45 NZ37
Shirley 24 SP17
Shirrell Heath 10 SU51
Shobdon 23 SO36
Shoeburyness 19 TQ98
Shoreham-by-Sea 11 TQ20
Shorne 12 TQ67
Shorwell 10 SZ48
Shotley 19 TM23
Shottisham 19 TM34
Shrawley 23 SO86
Shrewsbury 30 SJ41
Shrewton 15 SU04
Shrivenham 15 SU28
Shurdington 24 SO91
Sible Hedingham 18 TL73
Sibsey 33 TF35
Sibson 24 SK30
Sidcup 12 TQ47
Sidmouth 8 SY18
Silchester 16 SU66
Silloth 43 NY15
Silver End 18 TL81
Silverdale 39 SD47
Silverstone 25 SP64
Silverton 7 SS90
Simonsbath 7 SS73
Singleton 11 SU81
Sittingbourne 13 TQ96
Six Mile Bottom 18 TL55
Skaill 67 HY50
Skeabost Bridge 58 NG44
Skegness 33 TF56
Skellow 36 SE51
Skelmersdale 34 SD40
Skelmorlie 51 NS16
Skenfrith 23 SO42
Skewen 21 SS79
Skipness 46 NR95
Skipsea 41 TA15
Skipton 35 SD90
Slaidburn 34 SD75
Slaithwaite 35 SE01
Slamannan 47 NS87
Slapton 8 SX84
Sleaford 33 TF04
Sledmere 41 SE96
Sliddery 46 NR92
Sligachan 58 NG43
Slimbridge 15 SO70
Slough 17 SU97
Smailholm 49 NT63
Small Dole 11 TQ21
Smallways 40 NZ11
Smethwick 24 SP08
Snainton 41 SE98
Snaith 36 SE62
Snape 19 TM35
Snarestone 31 SK30
Snetterton 27 TM08
Snodland 12 TQ76
Solihull 24 SP17
Somerford 30 SJ86
Somersham 26 TL37
Somerton 14 ST42
Sonning 16 SU77
Sorbie 42 NX44
Sorisdale 50 NM26
Sorn 47 NS52
Soulby 39 NY71
Sourton 5 SX58
South Benfleet 18 TQ78
South Brent 8 SX66
South Godstone 12 TQ34
South Harting 11 SU71
South Kilworth 25 SP68
South Lopham 27 TM08
South Milton 5 SX74
South Mimms 17 TL20
South Molton 6 SS72
South Normanton 31 SK45
South Ockendon 12 TQ58
South Otterington 40 SE38
South Petherton 9 ST41
South Queensferry 48 NT17
South Raynham 26 TF82
South Shields 45 NZ36
South Walsham 27 TG31
South Wigston 25 SP59
South Woodham Ferrers.. 18 TQ89
South Zeal 5 SX69
Southall 17 TQ18
Southam 24 SP46
Southampton 10 SU41
Southborough 12 TQ54
Southbourne 11 SU70
Southend-on-Sea 19 TQ88

Southgate 17 TQ29
Southminster 19 TQ99
Southmoor 16 SU39
Southport 34 SD31
Southrepps 27 TG23
Southsea 11 SZ69
Southwell 32 SK75
Southwick 12 TQ20
Southwold 27 TM57
Sowerby Bridge 35 SE02
Sowton 8 SX99
Spalding 33 TF22
Sparkford 15 ST62
Spean Bridge 55 NN28
Speke 30 SJ48
Spencers Wood 16 SU76
Spennymoor 45 NZ23
Spey Bay 62 NJ36
Spilsby 33 TF46
Spratton 25 SP77
Springhead 35 SD90
Square and Compass 20 SN10
Stanton 26 TL97
St Abbs 49 NT96
St Agnes 4 SW75
St Albans 17 TL10
St Andrew 17 GN00
St Andrews 53 NO51
St Arvans 14 ST59
St Asaph 29 SJ07
St Aubin 9 JS00
St Austell 4 SX05
St Bees 38 NX91
St Blazey 5 SX05
St Boswells 48 NT53
St Brelade 9 JS00
St Brelade's Bay 9 JS00
St Breward 5 SX07
St Brides 20 SM81
St Clears 20 SN21
St Cleer 5 SX26
St Clement's Bay 9 JS00
St Combs 63 NK06
St Cyrus 57 NO76
St David's 20 SN21
St Day 4 SW74
St Dogmael's 20 SN14
St Fergus 63 NK05
St Fillans 52 NN62
St Helens 34 SJ59
St Helens 11 SZ68
St Helier 9 JS00
St Ives 4 SW54
St Ives 26 TL37
St John 9 JS00
St John's Chapel 45 NY83
St John's 38 SC28
St Judes 38 SC49
St Just 4 SW33
St Keverne 4 SW72
St Lawrence 9 JS00
St Lawrence 10 SZ57
St Leonards 10 SU10
St Leonards-on-Sea 12 TQ80
St Margaret's Hope 67 ND49
St Margarets Bay 13 TR34
St Mark's 38 SC37
St Martin 9 GN00
St Martin 9 JS00
St Mary Church 7 ST07
St Mary's 9 JS00
St Mary's Bay 13 TR02
St Mary's Loch 48 NT22
St Marychurch 8 SX96
St Marys 67 HY40
St Mawes 4 SW83
St Mawgan 4 SW86
St Mellion 5 SX36
St Michael's on Wyre 34 SD44
St Monans 53 NO50
St Neot 5 SX16
St Neots 25 TL16
St Nicholas at Wade 13 TR26
St Ouen 9 JS00
St Peter 9 JS00
St Peter Port 9 GN00
St Sampson 9 GN00
St Saviour 9 JS00
St Teath 5 SX08
St Wenn 4 SW96
Stadhampton 16 SU69
Staffin 58 NG46
Stafford 30 SJ92
Staindrop 40 NZ12
Staines 17 TQ07
Stainforth 39 SD86
Staithes 41 NZ71

Stalham	27	TG32
Stalybridge	35	SJ99
Stamford Bridge	41	SE75
Stamford	33	TF00
Standish	34	SD51
Standlake	16	SP30
Stanhope	45	NY93
Stanley	52	NO13
Stanley	45	NZ15
Stanmore	17	TQ19
Stansted	18	TL52
Stanstead Abbotts	18	TL31
Stanton Harcourt	16	SP40
Stanton	27	TL97
Stanway	24	SP03
Stapleford	32	SK43
Staplehurst	12	TQ74
Starcross	8	SX98
Starkigarth	63	HU42
Staunton	23	SO51
Staveley	31	SK47
Staverton	8	SX76
Staxton	41	TA07
Steeple Aston	24	SP42
Steeple Bumpstead	18	TL64
Steeton	35	SE04
Stein	58	NG25
Stelling Minnis	13	TR14
Stepaside	20	SN10
Stepps	47	NS66
Stevenage	17	TL22
Stevenston	46	NS24
Stewarton	47	NS44
Stibb Cross	6	SS41
Stickney	33	TF35
Stilligarry	64	NF73
Stillington	40	SE56
Stilton	25	TL18
Stirling	52	NS79
Stockbridge	10	SU33
Stockport	35	SJ88
Stocksbridge	35	SK29
Stockton Heath	30	SJ68
Stockton-on-Tees	40	NZ41
Stoer	64	NC02
Stogursey	14	ST24
Stoke Canon	8	SX99
Stoke Ferry	26	TF70
Stoke Fleming	8	SX84
Stoke Gabriel	8	SX85
Stoke Goldington	25	SP84
Stoke Holy Cross	27	TG20
Stoke Mandeville	16	SP81
Stoke Poges	16	SU98
Stoke-by-Nayland	19	TL93
Stoke-on-Trent	30	SJ84
Stokenchurch	16	SU79
Stokesley	40	NZ50
Ston Easton	15	ST65
Stone	30	SJ93
Stonehaven	57	NO88
Stonehouse	15	SO80
Stoneykirk	42	NX05
Stonor	16	SU78
Stornoway	64	NB43
Storrington	11	TQ01
Stotfold	18	TL23
Stourbridge	24	SO98
Stourport-on-Severn	23	SO87
Stourton	23	SO88
Stow Cum Quy	18	TL56
Stow	48	NT44
Stow-on-the-Wold	24	SP12
Stowmarket	19	TM05
Strachan	57	NO69
Strachur	51	NN00
Stradbroke	27	TM27
Stradishall	18	TL75
Stradsett	26	TF60
Straiton	47	NS30
Stranraer	42	NX06
Stratford	18	TQ38
Stratford-upon-Avon	24	SP25
Strath Kanaird	65	NC10
Strathaven	47	NS74
Strathblane	52	NS57
Strathcarron	59	NG94
Strathdon	57	NJ31
Strathmiglo	53	NO21
Strathpeffer	60	NH45
Strathtummel	56	NN86
Strathy	66	NC86
Strathyre	52	NN51
Stratton	6	SS20
Streatham	17	TQ27
Streatley	16	SU58
Street	14	ST43
Streetly	24	SP09
Strensall	40	SE66
Strete	8	SX84
Stretford	35	SJ79
Stretham	26	TL57
Stretton	30	SJ68
Stretton	32	SK91
Strichen	63	NJ95
Stromeferry	59	NG83
Stromness	67	HY20
Stronachlachar	51	NN41
Strone	51	NS18
Strontian	54	NM86
Strood	12	TQ76
Stroud	15	SO80
Struan	58	NG33
Struy	60	NH43
Studland	10	SZ08
Studley	24	SP06
Sturminster Newton	9	ST71
Sturton	32	SK88
Sudbury	31	SK13
Sudbury	19	TL84
Sulby	38	SC39
Sullom Voe	63	HU47
Sumburgh	63	HU40
Summercourt	4	SW85
Sunbury-on-Thames	17	TQ16
Sunderland	45	NZ35
Surbiton	17	TQ16
Sutterton	33	TF23
Sutton Benger	15	ST97
Sutton Coldfield	24	SP19
Sutton Scotney	10	SU43
Sutton	12	TQ26
Sutton Veny	15	ST84
Sutton upon Derwent	36	SE74
Sutton Valence	12	TQ84
Sutton-in-Ashfield	32	SK45
Sutton-on-Sea	33	TF58
Sutton-on-the-Forest	40	SE56
Sutton-on-Trent	32	SK76
Swadlincote	31	SK31
Swaffham	26	TF80
Swainswick	15	ST76
Swalcliffe	24	SP33
Swallowfield	16	SU76
Swanage	10	SZ07
Swanley	12	TQ56
Swansea	21	SS69
Sway	10	SZ29
Swaythling	10	SU41
Swillington	36	SE33
Swindon	15	SU18
Swineshead	33	TF24
Swineshead	25	TL06
Swinton	49	NT84
Swinton	36	SK49
Syderstone	26	TF83
Symbister	63	HU56
Symington	48	NS93
Symonds Yat	23	SO51
Synod	21	SN45
Syre	66	NC64
Syston	32	SK61
Tadcaster	36	SE44
Tadley	16	SU56
Tadworth	12	TQ25
Taff's Well	14	ST18
Tain	61	NH78
Tal-y-Bont	28	SH76
Tal-y-Cafn	29	SH77
Tal-y-Llyn	28	SH70
Talgarreg	21	SN45
Talgarth	22	SO13
Talke	30	SJ85
Talladale	59	NG97
Talland Bay	5	SX25
Talsarnau	28	SH63
Talybont	22	SN68
Talybont-on-Usk	22	SO12
Tamworth	24	SK20
Tan-y-Groes	20	SN24
Tangusdale	64	NF60
Tankerton	13	TR16
Tannadice	53	NO45
Taplow	16	SU98
Tarbert	58	NB10
Tarbert	51	NR86
Tarbet	51	NN30
Tarbolton	47	NS42
Tarfside	57	NO47
Tarland	57	NJ40
Tarleton	34	SD42
Tarporley	30	SJ56
Tarrant Keyneston	9	ST90
Tarskavaig	58	NG50
Tarves	62	NJ83
Taunton Deane S A	7	ST12
Taunton	14	ST22
Tavistock	5	SX47
Tayinloan	46	NR74
Taynuilt	55	NN03
Tayport	53	NO42
Tayvallich	50	NR78
Teangue	58	NG60
Tedburn St Mary	8	SX89
Teddington	17	TQ17
Teesside Airport	40	NZ31
Teignmouth	8	SX97
Telford	30	SJ60
Temple Bar	21	SN55
Temple Ewell	13	TR24
Temple	48	NT35
Temple Sowerby	39	NY62
Templecombe	15	ST72
Templeton	20	SN11
Tenbury Wells	23	SO56
Tenby	20	SN10
Tenterden	13	TQ83
Tern Hill	30	SJ63
Tetbury	15	ST89
Tetford	33	TF37
Teviothead	44	NT40
Tewkesbury	23	SO83
Thakeham	11	TQ11
Thame	16	SP70
Thames Ditton	17	TQ16
Thatcham	16	SU56
Thaxted	18	TL63
The Barringtons	24	SP21
The Bungalow	38	SC38
The Lhen	38	NX30
Theale	16	SU67
Thetford	26	TL88
Theydon Bois	18	TQ49
Thingwall	29	SJ28
Thirlspot	38	NY31
Thirsk	40	SE48
Thornbury	15	ST69
Thorne	36	SE61
Thorney	26	TF20
Thorngumbald	37	TA22
Thornhill	52	NS69
Thornhill	43	NX89
Thornley	45	NZ33
Thornthwaite	38	NY22
Thornton Dale	41	SE88
Thornton Heath	17	TQ36
Thornton Hough	29	SJ38
Thornton	34	SD30
Thornton	34	SD34
Thornton Watlass	40	SE28
Thornton-le-Street	40	SE48
Thorpe Bay	13	TQ98
Thorpe Market	27	TG23
Thorpe	31	SK15
Thorpe Thewles	40	NZ32
Thorpe-le-Soken	19	TM12
Thorpeness	19	TM45
Thorverton	7	SS90
Thrapston	25	SP97
Three Cocks	22	SO13
Three Legged Cross	10	SU00
Threekingham	33	TF03
Threlkeld	38	NY32
Threshfield	39	SD96
Thropton	45	NU00
Throwleigh	5	SX69
Thrumster	67	ND34
Thrussington	32	SK61
Thurcroft	36	SK48
Thurlaston	24	SP47
Thurlestone	5	SX64
Thurmaston	32	SK60
Thurnby	25	SK60
Thurnscoe	36	SE40
Thursby	44	NY35
Thurso	67	ND16
Thwaite	39	SD89
Tickenham	14	ST47
Tickhill	36	SK59
Ticknall	31	SK32
Tideford	5	SX35
Tideswell	31	SK17
Tigharry	64	NF77
Tighnabruaich	51	NR97
Tilbury	12	TQ67
Tilford	11	SU84
Tillicoultry	52	NS99
Tilshead	15	SU04
Tilton	32	SK70

Timperley ... 35 SJ78
Tintagel ... 5 SX08
Tintern ... 14 SO50
Tintinhull ... 9 ST41
Tintwistle ... 35 SK09
Tipton ... 24 SO99
Tiptree ... 19 TL81
Titchfield ... 10 SU50
Titchwell ... 26 TF74
Tiverton ... 7 SS91
Tividale ... 24 SO99
Tobermory ... 54 NM55
Tockwith ... 36 SE45
Toddington ... 25 TL02
Todmorden ... 35 SD92
Todwick ... 32 SK48
Tollerton ... 32 SK63
Tollesbury ... 19 TL91
Tolleshunt D'Arcy ... 19 TL91
Tolworth ... 17 TQ16
Tomatin ... 61 NH72
Tomdoun ... 55 NH10
Tomich ... 60 NH32
Tomintoul ... 56 NJ11
Tomnavoulin ... 61 NJ22
Ton Pentre ... 21 SS99
Tonbridge ... 12 TQ54
Tongue ... 66 NC55
Tonypandy ... 14 SS99
Tonyrefail ... 14 ST08
Topcliffe ... 40 SE47
Topsham ... 8 SX98
Torcross ... 8 SX84
Tore ... 60 NH55
Tormarton ... 15 ST77
Torness ... 60 NH52
Torphins ... 57 NJ60
Torpoint ... 5 SX45
Torquay ... 8 SX96
Torrance ... 47 NS67
Torridon ... 59 NG95
Torrin ... 58 NG52
Torthorwald ... 43 NY07
Torver ... 38 SD29
Totland Bay ... 10 SZ38
Totnes ... 8 SX86
Tottington ... 35 SD71
Totton ... 10 SU31
Tow Law ... 45 NZ13
Towcester ... 25 SP64
Tranent ... 48 NT47
Tranmere ... 29 SJ38
Traquair ... 48 NT33
Trawsfynydd ... 28 SH73
Trearddur Bay ... 28 SH27
Trebetherick ... 4 SW97
Trecastle ... 22 SN82
Tredegar ... 14 SO10
Treekingham ... 32 TF03
Trefriw ... 29 SH76
Tregaron ... 21 SN65
Tregony ... 4 SW94
Treherbert ... 21 SS99
Trelights ... 4 SW97
Trelleck ... 14 SO50
Tremadog ... 28 SH54
Treorchy ... 14 SS99
Trevor ... 29 SJ24
Treyarnon Bay ... 4 SW87
Trimdon ... 45 NZ33
Trimingham ... 27 TG23
Tring ... 17 SP91
Trinity ... 9 JS00
Troon ... 47 NS33
Trotton ... 11 SU82
Troutbeck ... 39 NY40
Trowbridge ... 15 ST85
Truro ... 4 SW84
Tummel Bridge ... 52 NN75
Tunbridge Wells ... 12 TQ53
Tunstall ... 19 TM35
Turnberry ... 46 NS20
Turners Hill ... 12 TQ33
Turriff ... 62 NJ74
Turton ... 35 SD71
Tutbury ... 31 SK22
Tuxford ... 32 SK77
Twatt ... 67 HY22
Tweedsmuir ... 48 NT02
Twickenham ... 17 TQ17
Two Bridges ... 5 SX67
Twycross ... 31 SK30
Twyford ... 10 SU42
Twyford ... 16 SU77
Tyldesley ... 34 SD60
Tyn-y-Cefn ... 29 SJ04
Tyndrum ... 55 NN33

Tynemouth ... 45 NZ36
Tynet ... 62 NJ36
Tywyn ... 22 SH50

Ubley ... 14 ST55
Uckfield ... 12 TQ42
Uddingston ... 47 NS66
Uffculme ... 7 ST01
Uffington ... 30 SJ51
Uig ... 64 NB03
Uig ... 58 NG36
Uldale ... 44 NY23
Ullapool ... 65 NH19
Ullesthorpe ... 24 SP58
Ulpha ... 38 SD19
Ulsta ... 63 HU47
Ulverston ... 38 SD27
Umberleigh ... 6 SS62
Unapool ... 65 NC23
Underbarrow ... 39 SD49
Union Mills ... 38 SC37
Upavon ... 15 SU15
Upermill ... 35 SD90
Uphall ... 48 NT07
Upholland ... 34 SD50
Uplyme ... 8 SY39
Upminster ... 18 TQ58
Upottery ... 8 ST20
Upper Gronant ... 29 SJ18
Upper Largo ... 53 NO40
Upper Slaughter ... 24 SP12
Uppingham ... 25 SP89
Upton ... 36 SE41
Upton upon Severn ... 23 SO84
Urmston ... 35 SJ79
Usk ... 14 SO30
Uttoxeter ... 31 SK03
Uxbridge ... 17 TQ08

Vale ... 17 GN00
Valley ... 28 SH27
Ventnor ... 10 SZ57
Verwood ... 10 SU00
Veryan ... 4 SW93
Vickerstown ... 38 SD16
Virkie ... 63 HU31
Voe ... 63 HU46

Waddington ... 35 SD74
Waddington ... 32 SK96
Wadebridge ... 4 SW97
Wadhurst ... 12 TQ63
Wainfleet ... 33 TF45
Wakefield ... 35 SE32
Walkden ... 35 SD70
Walkerburn ... 48 NT33
Walkington ... 37 SE93
Wall ... 45 NY96
Wallasey ... 34 SJ29
Wallingford ... 16 SU68
Wallington ... 17 TQ26
Walls ... 63 HU24
Wallsend ... 45 NZ26
Wallyford ... 48 NT37
Walmer ... 13 TR35
Walsall ... 24 SP09
Walsden ... 35 SD92
Waltham Abbey ... 18 TL30
Waltham Cross ... 17 TL30
Waltham ... 37 TA20
Waltham-on-the-Wolds ... 32 SK82
Walthamstow ... 17 TQ38
Walton ... 23 SO25
Walton-on-Thames ... 17 TQ16
Walton-on-the-Naze ... 19 TM22
Wamphray ... 43 NY19
Wandsworth ... 17 TQ27
Wanlockhead ... 47 NS81
Wansford ... 25 TL09
Wantage ... 16 SU48
Warboys ... 26 TL38
Warburton ... 34 SJ78
Warcop ... 39 NY71
Ware ... 17 TL31
Wareham ... 9 SY98
Wargrave ... 16 SU77
Wark ... 44 NY87
Warkworth ... 45 NU20
Warmington ... 24 SP44
Warminster ... 15 ST84
Warmley ... 15 ST67
Warmsworth ... 36 SE50
Warrington ... 34 SJ68
Warsash ... 10 SU40

Warsop ... 32 SK56
Warton ... 34 SD42
Warwick ... 24 SP26
Wasbister ... 67 HY33
Wasdale Head ... 38 NY10
Wasdale ... 38 NY10
Washingborough ... 32 TF07
Washington ... 45 NZ35
Watchet ... 7 ST04
Waterbeach ... 11 SU80
Watergate Bay ... 4 SW86
Wateringbury ... 12 TQ65
Waterlooville ... 11 SU60
Watermillock ... 39 NY42
Watford ... 17 TQ19
Wath-upon-Dearne ... 36 SE40
Watlington ... 16 SU69
Watnall ... 32 SK44
Watten ... 67 ND25
Watton ... 26 TF90
Watton-at-Stone ... 17 TL21
Wealdstone ... 17 TQ18
Weare ... 14 ST45
Wearhead ... 44 NY83
Weaverham ... 30 SJ67
Wedmore ... 14 ST44
Wednesbury ... 24 SO99
Wednesfield ... 24 SJ90
Weedon ... 25 SP65
Weldon ... 25 SP98
Welford ... 25 SP68
Wellesbourne ... 24 SP25
Welling ... 12 TQ47
Wellingborough ... 25 SP86
Wellington ... 30 SJ61
Wellington ... 7 ST12
Wells ... 14 ST54
Wells-next-the-Sea ... 26 TF94
Welney ... 26 TL59
Welshampton ... 30 SJ43
Welshpool ... 29 SJ20
Welwyn Garden City ... 17 TL21
Wem ... 30 SJ52
Wembley ... 17 TQ18
Wembury ... 5 SX54
Wemyss Bay ... 51 NS16
Wendover ... 16 SP80
Wensley ... 40 SE08
Wentbridge ... 36 SE41
Weobley ... 23 SO45
West Aukland ... 40 NZ12
West Bergholt ... 19 TL92
West Bexington ... 9 SY58
West Bilney ... 26 TF71
West Bromwich ... 24 SP09
West Byfleet ... 17 TQ06
West Calder ... 48 NT06
West Chiltington ... 11 TQ01
West Coker ... 9 ST51
West Haddon ... 25 SP67
West Harptree ... 14 ST55
West Horsley ... 11 TQ05
West Kilbride ... 46 NS24
West Kirby ... 29 SJ28
West Lavington ... 15 SU05
West Linton ... 48 NT15
West Lulworth ... 9 SY88
West Meon ... 11 SU62
West Mersea ... 19 TM01
West Molesey ... 17 TQ16
West Moors ... 10 SU00
West Pentire ... 4 SW76
West Quantoxhead ... 7 ST14
West Runton ... 27 TG14
West Thurrock ... 12 TQ57
West Wellow ... 10 SU21
West Wickham ... 12 TQ36
West Wittering ... 11 SZ79
West Witton ... 40 SE08
West Woodburn ... 45 NY88
Westbury ... 30 SJ30
Westbury ... 15 ST85
Westbury Sub Mendip ... 14 ST54
Westbury-upon-Severn ... 23 SO71
Westcliff-on-Sea ... 12 TQ88
Westerdale ... 67 ND15
Westerham ... 12 TQ45
Westgate-on-Sea ... 13 TR37
Westhill ... 57 NJ80
Westhoughton ... 34 SD60
Westleton ... 19 TM46
Westlinton ... 18 TL23
Weston ... 30 SJ52
Weston ... 31 SJ92
Weston-Super-Mare ... 14 ST36
Weston-in-Gordano ... 14 ST47
Weston-on-the-Green ... 16 SP51

95

Weston-under-Lizard	30	SJ81
Westonbirt	15	ST88
Westward Ho!	6	SS42
Wetheral	44	NY45
Wetherby	36	SE44
Wethersfield	18	TL73
Weybourne	27	TG14
Weybridge	17	TQ06
Weymouth	9	SY67
Whaley Bridge	31	SK08
Whalley	35	SD73
Whauphill	42	NX44
Wheathampstead	17	TL11
Wheddon Cross	7	SS93
Whickham	45	NZ26
Whiddon Down	5	SX49
Whimple	8	SY09
Whippingham	10	SZ59
Whipsnade	17	TL01
Whitburn	47	NS96
Whitburn	45	NZ46
Whitby	41	NZ81
Whitchurch	30	SJ54
Whitchurch	23	SO51
Whitchurch	16	SP82
Whitchurch	10	SU44
Whitebridge	60	NH41
Whitebrook	14	SO50
Whitefield	35	SD80
Whitehall	67	HY62
Whitehaven	38	NX91
Whitehills	62	NJ66
Whitemoor	4	SW95
Whiteness	63	HU34
Whitestone	23	SO54
Whithorn	42	NX44
Whiting Bay	46	NS02
Whitland	20	SN21
Whitley Bay	45	NZ37
Whitney-on-Wye	23	SO24
Whitstable	13	TR16
Whittington	29	SJ33
Whittle le Woods	34	SD52
Whittlesey	26	TL29
Whitton	23	SO26
Whitwell	10	SZ57
Whitwell-on-the-Hill	41	SE76
Whitworth	35	SD81
Wick	67	ND35
Wickford	18	TQ79
Wickham Market	19	TM35
Wickham	10	SU51
Wickwar	15	ST78
Widdrington	45	NZ29
Widecombe in the Moor	8	SX77
Widemouth Bay	6	SS20
Widmerpool	32	SK62
Widnes	30	SJ58
Wigan	34	SD50
Wigston	25	SP69
Wigton	44	NY24
Wigtown	42	NX45
Wilkieston	48	NT16
Willenhall	24	SO99
Willerby	37	TA03
Willersey	24	SP13
Willersley	23	SO34
Willingham	26	TL47
Willington	45	NZ13
Williton	7	ST04
Wilmcote	24	SP15
Wilmington	8	SY29
Wilmslow	30	SJ88
Wilsontown	47	NS95
Wilton	15	SU03
Wimbledon	17	TQ27
Wimborne Minster	10	SZ09
Wincanton	15	ST72
Winchelsea	13	TQ91
Winchester	10	SU42
Windermere	39	SD49
Windsor	17	SU97
Wing	16	SP82
Wingham	13	TR25
Winkleigh	6	SS60
Winnard's Perch	4	SW96
Winnersh	16	SU77
Winscombe	14	ST45
Winsford	30	SJ66
Winsford	7	SS93
Winslow	25	SP72
Winston	40	NZ11
Winterbourne Abbas	9	SY69
Winterbourne Whitechurch	9	ST80
Winterton-on-Sea	27	TG41
Wirksworth	31	SK25
Wisbech	33	TF40
Wishaw	47	NS75
Wishaw	24	SP19
Witham	18	TL81
Withern	33	TF48
Withernsea	37	TA32
Witherslack	39	SD48
Withleigh	7	SS91
Withybrook	24	SP48
Withypool	7	SS83
Witney	16	SP30
Witton-le-Wear	45	NZ13
Wiveliscombe	7	ST02
Wix	19	TM12
Woburn	25	SP93
Woburn Sands	25	SP93
Woking	17	TQ05
Wokingham	16	SU86
Wolsingham	45	NZ03
Wolverhampton	24	SO99
Wolviston	40	NZ42
Wombwell	36	SE30
Wooburn Common	16	SU98
Wooburn Green	16	SU98
Woodbridge	19	TM24
Woodchurch	13	TQ93
Woodford Bridge	6	SS31
Woodford Green	18	TQ39
Woodhead	35	SK09
Woodingdean	12	TQ30
Woodlands	36	SE50
Woodlands	10	SU31
Woodstock	16	SP41
Woodville	31	SK31
Woody Bay	6	SS64
Woofferton	23	SO56
Wool	9	SY88
Woolacombe	6	SS44
Wooler	49	NT92
Woolfardisworthy	6	SS32
Woolverton	15	ST75
Woore	30	SJ74
Wootton Bassett	15	SU08
Wootton Bridge	10	SZ59
Wootton	10	SZ59
Wootton	37	TA01
Worcester	23	SO85
Worcester Park	17	TQ26
Worfield	23	SO79
Workington	38	NX92
Worksop	32	SK57
Wormit	53	NO32
Worplesdon	17	SU95
Worsley	35	SD70
Worthing	11	TQ10
Wortley	35	SK39
Wortwell	27	TM28
Wotton-under-Edge	15	ST79
Wragby	33	TF17
Wrangaton	8	SX65
Wrangle	33	TF45
Wrea Green	34	SD33
Wrelton	41	SE78
Wrentham	27	TM48
Wrexham	29	SJ35
Writtle	18	TL60
Wrotham Heath	12	TQ65
Wroxall	10	SZ58
Wroxham	27	TG21
Wroxton	24	SP44
Wychbold	24	SO96
Wykeham	41	SE98
Wymondham	32	SK81
Wymondham	27	TG10
Yalding	12	TQ64
Yarcombe	8	ST20
Yardley Hastings	25	SP85
Yarm	40	NZ41
Yarrow	48	NT32
Yate	15	ST78
Yateley	16	SU86
Yattendon	16	SU57
Yatton Keynell	15	ST87
Yaxley	27	TM17
Yeadon	35	SE24
Yealmpton	5	SX55
Yelland	6	SS43
Yelverton	5	SX56
Yelverton	27	TG20
Yeovil	9	ST51
Yetholm	49	NT82
Yetts O'Muckhart	52	NO00
York	36	SE65
Youlgrave	31	SK26
Yoxall	31	SK11
Yoxford	19	TM36
Ysbyty Ystwyth	22	SN77
Ystalyfera	21	SN70
Ystrad Mynach	14	ST19
Ystradgynlais	21	SN71
Zeals	15	ST73
Zelah	4	SW85
Zennor	4	SW43

96